LOEB CLASSICAL MONOGRAPHS

❧ ❧ ❧ ❧

In Memory of
James C. Loeb

GREEK
TEXTUAL
CRITICISM
A Reader

Robert Renehan

❧ ❧ ❧ ❧

HARVARD UNIVERSITY PRESS

CAMBRIDGE, MASSACHUSETTS · 1969

The Loeb Classical Monographs are published
with assistance from the Loeb Classical Library
Foundation.

Library of Congress Catalog Card Number 72–82297

SBN 674–36310–8

Printed in the United States of America

IOANNAE
UXORI ADAMATAE

ὄστρακα
ἀντὶ
χρυσωμάτων

ACKNOWLEDGMENTS

Much of this book was written during the summer months of 1968; I should like to express my thanks to Boston College, which awarded me a summer grant at that time. The bulk of the typing was done by two of my students, Mr. Philip Cleary and Mr. Stanley Ragalevsky; they handled a tortuous, multilingual manuscript with unusual accuracy. Additions to the manuscript were typed by Mrs. Lillian Reisman, secretary to the Department of Classics at Boston College, with her customary efficiency.

I have discussed elsewhere several of the passages treated below; for permission to reprint (sometimes in a revised form) certain discussions I am grateful to the editors of *Classical Philology*, *Harvard Studies in Classical Philology*, *Philologus*, and *Rheinisches Museum für Philologie*. Professor Benedict Einarson of the University of Chicago very courteously criticized the typescript for the Harvard University Press; with his consent I am pleased to incorporate several of his comments into the text (they have been placed between brackets and signalized by the initials B.E.). The Harvard University Press did me an especial kindness in asking Mrs. Cedric Whitman as editor to see the work through the press: her exceptional learning has been familiar to me since the days when we were συμμαθηταί. Professor Bruno Snell graciously answered by letter several inquiries of mine on the text of Pindar. For this I respectfully record my thanks; to set down words in praise of a scholar of his stature would be an impertinence on my part.

Finally, the book, with all its inadequacies and faults, is my own child and no one else's; like the Greek or Roman father of old I must lift it up and acknowledge it. It may be that no one would care to dispute the parentage with me. Nevertheless, like any other child, it has grandparents to boast of, and I would be both disloyal and dishonest were I not to mention two scholars here: the Reverend Carl J. Thayer, S.J., who taught me to read the Greek language, and the late Werner Jaeger, who taught me philological method. In offering this little book to the public I do so with a devout prayer to God that it be judged not unworthy of these two honorable names.

Boston College   R.R.

CONTENTS

GREEK TEXTUAL CRITICISM

ἃ γὰρ δεῖ μαθόντας ποιεῖν, ταῦτα ποιοῦντες μανθάνομεν.

Aristoteles

τὸ γὰρ ἀκριβὲς οὐχ ὁμοίως ἐν ἅπασι τοῖς λόγοις ἐπιζητητέον.

Aristoteles

πάντα διάφορα ἐόντα ἀποκωλύει μὴ δυνατὸν εἶναι ἐς ἀκριβείην συγγραφῆναι.

"Hippocrates"

ἡ γὰρ τῶν λόγων κρίσις πολλῆς ἐστι πείρας τελευταῖον ἐπιγέννημα.

"Longinus"

A Foreword

The following essay on textual criticism must, in the last analysis, itself justify its *raison d'être*. However, to preclude any misconceptions, it has seemed advisable to state here exactly what I have attempted to do. The textual critic is the product of experience, of trial-and-error practice; a man can no more, simply by reading a tidy manual on textual criticism, acquire this craft than he can become a poet by conning an *ars poetica*. This essay makes no claims of being such a manual. It is intended to be a workbook, not a handbook. I have tried to show the textual critic actually at work on a number of specific passages where there is genuine doubt about what the author originally wrote. A good textual critic, in practicing his craft, follows a definite philological $\mu\acute{\epsilon}\theta o\delta o\varsigma$ which, by its nature, does not readily submit to rigid categories or to absolute rules set forth *in abstracto*. This explains the format of my essay; the reader will look in vain for chapter divisions or neat classifications of any sort. Any given textual problem may involve a variety of factors, all of which must be considered in determining the reading most likely to be correct; each passage ought to be regarded as a distinct entity which deserves an individual judgment. This situation renders any overly precise schematism both artificial and unrealistic. My procedure has been merely to set forth in sequence a selection of typical examples of textual problems and discuss them in detail. (The professional textual critic may find my discussions in places too detailed and obvious; I would ask him to remember that my purpose is to analyze complex processes for an audience not already fully conversant with them.) Passages exhibiting similar difficulties have of course been grouped together where feasible, but it will soon be apparent that no absolute order has been followed. The first impression may be one of formlessness; it was my own conviction, upon completion of this essay, that I had adopted the most realistic format for a work of this nature. The reader must judge that for himself.

A Foreword

The basic task of the textual critic is to determine, so far as is possible, the actual words of an author. To do this he has to make certain choices. He must decide in each case whether the original reading has been preserved (or conjecturally restored) in any MS tradition. If in his judgment it has not, he must decide whether it has been or can be recovered by modern conjecture or whether the passage is a *locus desperatus*. He must be willing to admit that in many instances certainty is not attainable. This essay is an attempt to show how the critic goes about, in practice, making those choices. It is primarily concerned, therefore, neither with stemmatics nor with paleography as such. To employ the terminology adopted by Paul Maas in his *Textual Criticism* (p. 1), this reader deals not with *recensio*, but with *examinatio*, including both *selectio* between variants and *divinatio*.

A word about conjectures is necessary. Many of the passages discussed depend for their solution upon conjectural emendation. This is so simply because I have had to choose as illustrations in most cases *cruces*—specifically those passages where something is amiss which needs to be set right by the critic. The reader must not take away the false impression that conjectural rewriting is the normal prerequisite for a satisfactory text. The MSS far more frequently than not preserve exactly what the author wrote; these cases usually require no discussion on the part of the textual critic. The examples in this reader, precisely because they are in good part examples of corruptions, are to that extent untypical; that is as it must be. Nor must the reader conceive that I have composed a manual of instructions on how to make an emendation. That ability cannot be taught, it must be innate. The skill of a Porson or Housman at remedying with an easy dispatch *crux* after *crux* ought indeed to be numbered among the θεῶν ἐρικυδέα δῶρα; not without reason has this faculty been called in the Latin tongue *divinatio*. The most ingenious critics, though, have not always been the soundest. The materials in this book have been put together with the hope that they may be of some help in developing a facility at making a reasonable and sound choice between possible readings, whether these possible readings be genuine MS lections or conjectures (ancient, medieval, or modern). This ability to choose soundly can be acquired;

it is founded upon wide and careful reading combined with a constant effort to refine one's sense of the probable. If not so splendid a talent as *divinatio*, it is a more useful one; the emendator, *qua* emendator, contributes to the explication of corrupt, that is to say untypical, passages. (I ought here to call attention to a widely held misconception: the belief that there are few "emendable" passages still left. Almost all corruptions, it is often maintained, have either been detected and corrected or are irremediable. This is simply not true. Of course, in the major classical authors the correct solutions for most of the corruptions have already been proposed [though it does not follow that these solutions will necessarily be found adopted in our current editions]. But even here work yet remains to be done. In less widely read authors, especially the postclassical ones, a very great number of passages still await their Oedipus.)

To conclude, the following essay, as I have indicated, attempts to show the textual critic at work; it is not an exercise in bibliography. It seemed to me neither necessary nor desirable to include a notice of everything that has been written about every passage discussed. Nor, for that matter, do I claim to have read all the modern scholarship. To attempt that would leave little time for reading that Greek and Latin literature, which alone justifies modern classical scholarship. I have tried to consult all the major editions, commentaries, lexica, and concordances; in the following pages silence on my part should by no means be construed as due in every instance to ignorance. Ultimately, however, this essay is the product of my own reading of the Greek texts and thinking about them; it is, essentially, not a derivative work. Wherever I have learned anything substantive to my argument from another scholar, I have acknowledged it. It is perhaps inevitable that some things which I think are my own have already been said by others. It is certainly inevitable that my judgment in some cases shall prove to be wrong. Fortunately, the value of this essay does not depend upon the correctness of my judgment in any given passage. I have consciously attempted, in the writing of these pages, to trace out what I believe to be a true philological μέθοδος. It is this method which is important; if I have been successful, it will gradually appear to the reader who carefully works his way through the examples.

Corrections and improvements, whether imparted by private communication or, more valuably, in print, I earnestly solicit and will gratefully accept, believing with Epicurus that ἐν φιλολόγῳ συζητήσει πλεῖον ἤνυσεν ὁ ἡττηθείς, καθ' ὃ προσέμαθεν.

§1. Euripides *Cyclops* 131

οἶσθ᾽ οὖν ὃ δράσεις, ὡς ἀπαίρωμεν χθονός;

A flawless verse; but it is probably not what Euripides wrote. Canter conjectured δρᾶσον for δράσεις and editors usually so print. In Euripides the expression οἶσθ᾽ οὖν ὃ δρᾶσον recurs at *Hel.* 315, 1233; *IA* 725; *Ion* 1029 (compare also *Heracl.* 451). The aorist imperative with οἶσθ᾽ ὅ is a common construction in the Attic dramatists but is apparently peculiar to them. δράσεις, therefore, in this passage is a *trivialization* caused by a misunderstanding of the construction. Here no trace of the true reading has survived in our MSS; in *Hecuba* 225 only part of the tradition was affected, so that we can still see quite clearly the genesis of the corruption. Here MP (and Gregory of Corinth, p. 17) have οἶσθ᾽ οὖν ὃ δρᾶσον; AL (and the first hand of M above the verse) give δράσεις for δρᾶσον; the scholiast comments τὰ καλὰ τῶν ἀντιγράφων δρᾶσον ἔχει. (Both Goodwin [*Greek Moods and Tenses*² 253] and LSJ s.v. εἴδω B.8 recognize οἶσθ᾽ οὖν ὃ δράσεις for *Cyc.* 131, wrongly in my judgment.) A similar example is *Med.* 600:

οἶσθ᾽ ὡς μετεύξῃ καὶ σοφωτέρα φανῇ;

Elmsley correctly saw that the future indicative μετεύξῃ was a corruption of the aorist imperative μέτευξαι. (The scholiast paraphrases οἶσθα ὥς σε ἔδει μετεύξασθαι, but this is inconclusive.) οἶσθ᾽ ὡς with the aorist imperative is another idiom proper to the Attic dramatists (compare also *IT* 1203 οἶσθα νῦν ἅ μοι γενέσθω). Here the presence of the future indicative φανῇ made the error especially easy. In Sophocles *OT* 543 οἶσθ᾽ ὡς πόησον the extant tradition lucidly reveals the error in the making. L, the most important MS, has πόησον, which was "corrected" to πόησων; the other MSS have ποιήσων. The scholiast and the *Suda*, s.v. οἶσθα, preserve πόησον. More than one factor may have caused the error: 1) The construction was misunderstood; 2) ο and ω had become identical in pronunciation (whence the names ὁ μικρόν and ὦ μέγα to distinguish them); 3) οἶδα and ὡς are both often con-

5

strued with a participle. Notice that in this example the MSS, apart from L, show a further corruption: ποιήσων (for the Attic ποή-). It is a general principle that the more common (orthography, word, phrase, construction, thought) tends to supplant the less common; such trivializations are legion. A balanced judgment of the frequency and probability of this type of error can best be acquired from wide reading of the MSS themselves, since the majority of such slips are normally (and rightly) not reported in critical editions.

§2. Euripides *Orestes* 1093–1094

τί γὰρ ἐρῶ κἀγώ ποτε
γῆν Δελφίδ᾽ ἐλθὼν Φωκέων ἀκρόπολιν . . .

ἀκρόπολιν is unmetrical; the correction is obvious and was made in the early editions: ἀκρόπτολιν. Similar instances are Hecuba 767 . . . ἡνίκ᾽ ὤλλυτο πτόλις (end of an iambic trimeter), where A and L wrongly have πόλις; Hecuba 1209 . . . πέριξ δὲ πύργος εἶχ᾽ ἔτι πτόλιν (end of a trimeter), where A (and OF?) has preserved πτόλιν against πόλιν of most MSS. In these examples meter pointed the corruption; where meter cannot be used as a touchstone, such trivializations must often remain undetected or doubtful.

§3. Euripides *Hecuba* 385–387

. . . τήνδε μὲν μὴ κτείνετε,
ἡμᾶς δ᾽ ἄγοντες πρὸς πυρὰν Ἀχιλλέως
κεντεῖτε . . .

In verse 387 V reads κτενεῖτε, an almost inevitable slip, both because of κτείνετε in verse 385 and because κτείνω is a far commoner word than κεντω.

6

§4. Plato *Symposium* 201C

οὐ μὲν οὖν τῇ ἀληθείᾳ, φάναι, ὦ φιλούμενε Ἀγάθων, δύνασαι
ἀντιλέγειν, ἐπεὶ Σωκράτει γε οὐδὲν χαλεπόν.

P. Oxy. 843 has φιλε for φιλούμενε. Paul Maas in his *Textual Criticism*,
p. 39, comments that "no one had noticed that φιλούμενος=φίλος is
singular. It is true the corruption remains unexplained." What is singular is not necessarily corrupt; here it is essential to examine the context.
Socrates, the speaker, has assumed a somewhat playful tone toward
Agathon, the distinguished tragic poet; he says ὦ φιλούμενε Ἀγάθων
because he is parodying tragic diction:

ἔστ᾽, ὦ φιληθεὶς ὡς σὺ νῦν ἐμοὶ φιλῇ

(Eur. *Hec.* 1000)

ἀλλ᾽, ὦ φιληθεῖσ᾽, ὦ κασίγνητον κάρα

(Eur. *IT* 983)

For the present participle compare a choral verse in Aristophanes
Pax 588: ἦσθα γὰρ μέγιστον ἡμῖν κέρδος, ὦ ποθουμένη. It is not impossible, but quite beyond demonstration, that in this sentence Plato
has parodied a specific verse or a mannerism of Agathon's. Several of
my students to whom I posed this passage as a problem suggested independently an attractive alternate defense of φιλούμενε: elsewhere in
the *Symposium* (174A, 213C) Agathon is represented as handsome,
καλός, κάλλιστος. This adjective is used explicitly of a παιδικά by his
lover; see my paper "Some Greek Lexicographical Notes," *Glotta* 46
(1968) 69. Possibly the "asexual" φιλούμενε here is a Socratic parody
modeled on the common term ἐρώμενος, which is quite specifically
sexual.

φιλούμενε is sound; φιλε of the papyrus is a simple case of the replacement of the uncommon by the common. I can provide a parallel in
Plato to the "singular" φιλούμενε, from which it may be seen how
lubricous objections on grounds of singularity really are. In a passage

in the *Phaedrus* (238D), Socrates states: τὰ νῦν γὰρ οὐκέτι πόρρω διθυράμβων φθέγγομαι; I cite this because it gives some idea of the tone of the context and its poetical coloration. Shortly thereafter Socrates exclaims: εἶεν ὦ φέριστε. Not only is the adjective φέριστος proper to poetic diction, but even in poetry it is of rarer occurrence than its by-form φέρτατος (though in the *vocative* φέριστε seems to be commoner). Ast in his *Lexicon Platonicum* (admittedly a not entirely reliable work) cites only the *Phaedrus* passage for φέριστε; I can cite no second instance of the adjective in Plato, nor for that matter in Greek prose. Despite this "singularity" no one has questioned ὦ φέριστε here; no one should. (Of course, the existence of a few more isolated instances of ὦ φέριστε in prose, if such there be, would not really affect the point I am making.) A second parallel is *Philebus* 53D1 ὦ Πρώταρχε φίλε; the position of φίλε *after* the proper name is apparently unique. Nevertheless editors generally have not deemed it necessary to tamper with the text.

The fact that φίλε is attested in a papyrus of the second century A.D., while the lection φιλούμενε is preserved only in the much later Byzantine MSS, is not decisive. That the oldest witness is necessarily the most trustworthy is a theory long since exploded. In the *Hellenica* of Xenophon 1.3.19 the MSS have ... καὶ Ἀναξίλαος ὃς ὑπαγόμενος θανάτου ὕστερον ἐν Λακεδαίμονι διὰ τὴν προδοσίαν ἀπέφυγεν ... LSJ s.v. ὑπάγω II correctly explain the idiom: "*bring* a person *before the judgement-seat* (the ὑπό refers to his being set *under* or *below* the judge) ... *ὑ. τινὰ θανάτου* on a capital charge ..." In the *Hellenica* ὑπάγειν is used in this sense at 2.3.28, 2.3.33, 2.3.38; the idiom ὑπάγειν θανάτου occurs at 2.3.12 and 5.4.24 (ὑπῆγον Pierson: ἀπῆγον MSS). There is no doubt that ὑπαγόμενος in 1.3.19 is sound; a papyrus of the third century A.D., which preserves this passage, has ἐπαγόμενος. (Marchant in his Oxford edition inexplicably prints ἐπαγόμενος here, while printing forms of ὑπάγειν in all the other passages cited. ἐπάγειν never bears the meaning required by the context.) Take another example; Euripides *Troiades* 884–886:

> ὦ γῆς ὄχημα κἀπὶ γῆς ἔχων ἕδραν,
> ὅστις ποτ᾽ εἶ σύ, δυστόπαστος εἰδέναι,

8

Ζεύς, εἴτ' ἀνάγκη φύσεος εἴτε νοῦς βροτῶν,
προσηυξάμην σε.

These verses must have been famous in antiquity; Clement of Alexandria (*Protr.* 2.25.3) cites the first two (from a *florilegium?*) and Sextus Empiricus twice quotes them (all four verses at p. 666.5, verses 885–887 at p. 219.1). Both writers have in verse 885 δυστόπαστος εἰσιδεῖν; this is clearly an ancient variant which goes back to at least the second century A.D. Sextus and Clement are independent witnesses for the lection εἰσιδεῖν; it thus has excellent credentials and any editor of Euripides must give it serious consideration. Paleography is of no help here, since, for a variety of reasons, either infinitive could have replaced the other. [ιδ and ειδ were pronounced identically; ΕΙC (ΕC) could have been accidentally omitted or added because of the preceding -ΟC (cf. *IA* 171; *El.* 1242; *Tr.* 991). Possible stages of corruption in either direction are: (a) εἰσιδεῖν→ἰδεῖν→εἰδέναι (*metri gratia*); (b) εἰδέναι→(εἰσειδέναι→) εἰσιδεῖν, dittography, pronunciation, and meter all influencing the corruption. Furthermore, ἰδεῖν and εἰδέναι are etymologically cognate, and mental confusion between "perceive physically" (ἰδεῖν) and "perceive mentally" (εἰδέναι) was undoubtedly a factor.] The reality is that the *ductus litterarum* is irrelevant here. The question to be asked is which verb better suits the context. The editors are unanimous, so far as I can determine, in printing εἰδέναι, and they are correct in so doing. What is wanted in this passage is a verb of intellectual apprehension; it has long been recognized that Euripides is here echoing various philosophical speculations current in the Athens of his time. The evidence for such a philosophical usage of εἰσορᾶν in Euripides or elsewhere is not forthcoming. On the other hand, a single Euripidean trimeter (frag. 480 Nauck) presents a sufficiently eloquent defense of εἰδέναι:

Ζεὺς ὅστις ὁ Ζεύς, οὐ γὰρ οἶδα πλὴν λόγῳ.

Once again the medieval MSS have preserved a genuine reading where ancient witnesses have failed to do so.

§5. Plato *Hippias Minor* 365D5

ἔσται ταῦτα· ἀλλ' ἐρώτα ἔμβραχυ ὅτι βούλει.

ἔμβραχυ T W : ἐν βραχεῖ F

The adverb ἔμβραχυ, combined with relative words (ὅστις, ὅπου, etc.) with the meaning "at all," "soever," is an Attic idiom. In this passage the sense wanted is "ask whatever you wish," not "ask what you wish in a few words." It is readily understandable how a medieval scribe could substitute the much commoner expression ἐν βραχεῖ for ἔμβραχυ; the reverse is improbable. ἔμβραχυ is a genuine *lectio difficilior*. The confusion was one of sound; υ and ει had come to be identical in pronunciation, so that ἔμβραχυ and ἐν βραχεῖ were almost indistinguishable. See also Plato *Gorgias* 457A7 (ἔμβραχυ BTP: ἐν βραχεῖ F et rec. t) and *Symposium* 217A2 (ἔμβραχυ Cobet: ἐν βραχεῖ BTW). ["This appears not so much a matter of confused pronunciation—υ (οι) was distinct from ι (ει, η) until the tenth century, according to E. H. Sturtevant, *The Pronunciation of Greek and Latin*[2], pp. 43–44—as a matter of syntax: ἐν (or ἐμ; it does not matter) βραχύ simply looked soloecistic to the scribe; ἐν took the dative." B.E. This is possible, but confusion of pronunciation cannot be excluded. Complete identification in sound of υ and ει may not have occurred before the middle of the tenth century in educated speech; the beginnings of the confusion are certainly older.] In this case it was important to keep in mind that ἔμβραχυ was, for the most part, a phrase current in the Attic period of the Greek language. Linguistic chronology is often a crucial factor in dealing with a textual passage. In Apollonius of Rhodes 3.758 the phrase ἐν γαυλῷ κέχυται occurs; among the scholia to Apollonius there is the following marginal note (p. 239.11 Wendel):

ἐν γαυλῷ: ἐν κάδῳ, ὃ καλεῖται βεδοῦριν.

γαυλός is familiar enough to the classical scholar; to many a Byzantine it would have been an old and strange poetic word, hence the need of explaining it by a current synonym. Both the meaning and form of βεδοῦριν may be puzzling to the classicist. Not without reason; it is in fact a *vox nihili*. Read βεδούρι⟨ο⟩ν; the word (= "water bucket") came into medieval Greek from the Slavic. Compare Constantine Porphyrogennetus *De Caerimoniis* 466.19: βεδούρια ἀργυρᾶ εἰς νερὸν δύο. ["May not βεδοῦριν be right? -ιον had long before been simplified in vulgar pronunciation to -ιν; compare the writing of *Martialis* or *Apollinaris* as Μαρτιάλιος, Ἀπολλινάριος." B.E. This simplification of -ιον to -ιν is indeed quite common in the Byzantine period (and earlier); my colleague, Mr. Clive Foss, refers me to A. N. Jannaris, *An Historical Greek Grammar*, no. 302 and Appendix iii.7. The conjecture βεδούρι⟨ο⟩ν ought, therefore, to be rejected. I leave my discussion of the passage exactly as I wrote it: my imperfect acquaintance with Byzantine Greek, which there stands exposed, is as good an illustration as any of the very point which I wish to make.]

§6. Plato *Apology* 22D

ἀλλ', ὦ ἄνδρες Ἀθηναῖοι, ταὐτόν μοι ἔδοξαν ἔχειν ἁμάρτημα
ὅπερ καὶ οἱ ποιηταὶ καὶ οἱ ἀγαθοὶ δημιουργοί—διὰ τὸ τὴν τέχ
νην καλῶς ἐξεργάζεσθαι ἕκαστος ἠξίου καὶ τἆλλα τὰ μέγιστα
σοφώτατος εἶναι—καὶ αὐτῶν αὕτη ἡ πλημμέλεια ἐκείνην τὴν
σοφίαν ἀποκρύπτειν.

ἀποκρύπτειν W : ἀποκρύπτει B : ἀπέκρυπτεν T, versio Armeniaca

ἀποκρύπτειν, the *lectio difficilior*, should be read here; the infinitive is governed by ἔδοξε to be supplied from ἔδοξαν above. The construction (partly because of the intervening clause διὰ τὸ ... εἶναι) was misunderstood; ἀπέκρυπτεν is a conscious attempt to "restore" grammar. ἀποκρύπτει is either an unconscious accommodation to the indicative because of the preceding nominative αὕτη ἡ πλημμέλεια or, like ἀπέκρυπτεν, a conscious change. Thus, on the assumption that ἀποκρύπτειν is the original reading, we not only get the required sense but can also explain the origin of both variants. Of these variants ἀποκρύπτει cannot be correct; the context demands a past tense (compare ἔδοξαν and ἠξίου). ἀπέκρυπτεν would make sense, but, if it were the correct reading, neither of the other variants could be explained. There is no reason, psychological or paleographical, which would account for the corruption of ἀπέκρυπτεν to either ἀποκρύπτειν or ἀποκρύπτει.

§7. Plato *Epistle* 7.337B-C

τοὺς δὴ κρατήσαντας ἀεὶ χρὴ . . . τούτους δὴ δεήσεσιν καὶ τι-
μαῖς ὅτι μεγίσταις οἴκοθεν μεταπέμψασθαι, μεταπεμψαμένους
δὲ ὀμόσαντας δεῖσθαι καὶ κελεύειν θεῖναι νόμους, μήτε νικήσα-
σιν μήτε νικηθεῖσιν νέμειν πλέον . . .

Richards correctly saw that νέμειν should be νεμεῖν. The infinitive is governed by ὀμόσαντας and in such constructions the future infinitive is regular, the present rare (*Greek Moods and Tenses*² 136). Compare Plato *Ap.* 35C, *Phaedr.* 236D-E, *Menex.* 245C, *Leges* 683D, 684A-B. Verbs with future forms similar to present forms are frequently miscopied in MSS; the present tense, being more common, tends to replace the future. The average nonspecialist is disposed (in part unconsciously) to accord to MSS the kind of authority that the average person grants the printed page. In this passage, νέμειν is possible Greek and not a few would no doubt retain it, simply because the MSS have it. Plato, however, used no accents; they were added later. Suppose we had Plato's own copy of the *Seventh Letter* and wished to edit it. The autograph copy would have NEMEIN *sine accentu*. ὄμνυμι normally governs a future infinitive and Plato's usage does not differ from the norm. No competent editor would hesitate for a moment; he would print νεμεῖν. [I have previously discussed this passage in *CP* 57 (1962) 109.] A similar ambiguity in *Apology* 39B has gone unnoticed:

καὶ νῦν ἐγὼ μὲν ἄπειμι ὑφ' ὑμῶν θανάτου δίκην ὀφλών, οὗτοι δ'
ὑπὸ τῆς ἀληθείας ὠφληκότες μοχθηρίαν καὶ ἀδικίαν. καὶ ἐγώ τε
τῷ τιμήματι ἐμμένω καὶ οὗτοι.

Editors print ἐμμένω with the MSS, but the future ἐμμενῶ is quite possibly correct. Note ἄπειμι and compare *Crito* 53A νῦν δὲ δὴ οὐκ ἐμμενεῖς τοῖς ὡμολογημένοις, where the future is guaranteed by the sense.

§8. Athenaeus 15.690F

... ὡς καὶ τὸ Μεγάλλειον· ὠνομάσθη γὰρ καὶ τοῦτο ἀπὸ Μεγάλλου τοῦ Σικελιώτου· οἱ δ᾽ Ἀθηναῖόν φασιν εἶναι τὸν Μέγαλλον.

Μεγάλλειον was a "perfumed unguent named after the inventor Megallos" (LSJ). The word is found chiefly in the comic poets (LSJ cite Aristophanes, Strattis, Pherecrates, Anaxandrides, Eubulus, and Amphis). Exotic words such as this one are especially liable to corruption and confusion with commoner words of similar appearance. Thus codex A of Athenaeus has μεγαλεῖον, C and E μεγάλλιον (a later hand in C adds προπαροξυτόνως). The trivialization of μεγάλλειον to μεγαλεῖον is due to a confusion with the adjective μεγαλεῖος—an adjective which would be familiar to later, i.e. Christian, copyists because of its occurrences in the *Septuaginta* and the Greek New Testament (for example *Act. Ap.* 2.11 τὰ μεγαλεῖα τοῦ θεοῦ). This confusion was further facilitated by the frequent orthographic fluctuation in MSS between -λ- and -λλ-. The same corruption to μεγαλεῖον is found in Theophrastus *De Odoribus* 29 and elsewhere. The similarity of the uncial letters Τ and Γ produced a different corruption; Aristophanes frag. 536 Kock runs as follows: μεταπέμπου νῦν ταῦτα σπουδῇ καὶ μύρον, εὕρημα Μεγάλλου. This fragment is preserved by Hesychius under the entry Μετάλλειον (*sic*) μύρον; there we read εὕρημα Μετάλλου. The error is not due to a medieval scribe; Hesychius' entries are arranged in an alphabetical order of sorts (κατὰ στοιχεῖον), so that it is certain that the corruption to Μετ- goes back to him (or rather to his source). The same misspelling occurs in the *Etymologicum Magnum*, p. 587.6–9, where however there is added ὁ καὶ διὰ τοῦ Γ̄ γράφει Ἀριστοφάνης Τελμισσεῦσιν. Ὧρος.

§9. Xenophon *Historia Graeca* 1.1.23

παρὰ δὲ Ἱπποκράτους τοῦ Μινδάρου ἐπιστολέως εἰς Λακεδαί-
μονα γράμματα πεμφθέντα ἑάλωσαν εἰς Ἀθήνας λέγοντα τάδε·
"Ἔρρει τὰ καλά . . .

ἔρρει τὰ καλά . . . "The beautiful things are gone"; hardly pertinent
in a Laconic military dispatch. Bergk set things right by correcting to
τὰ κᾶλα, "the ships." κᾶλον is not a common word and trivialization
was inevitable; the same slip happened in Aristophanes *Lys.* 1253.
Similarly, forms of κάλως (κάλος in Epic and Ionic), "reefing rope,"
tend to be confused with forms of καλός.

§10. Apollonius Rhodius *Argonautica* 2.244–245

Ἆ δείλ᾽, οὔ τινά φημι σέθεν στυγερώτερον ἄλλον
ἔμμεναι ἀνθρώπων.

Zetes is here addressing his uncle Phineus in tones of compassion;
στυγερώτερον therefore does not seem apt. Ruhnken restored the true
reading σμυγερώτερον, which is confirmed by the gloss ἐπιπονέστερον
preserved in codices L and A. Compare 2.374 σμυγερώτατοι ἀνδρῶν
(where L and P annotate ἐπιπονέστατοι). In Sophocles *Philoctetes* 165–
166 θηροβολοῦντα πτηνοῖς ἰοῖς στυγερὸν στυγερῶς, Brunck conjectured σμυγερὸν σμυγερῶς. This is a doubtful case and editors are
divided. In support of Brunck's conjecture is the scholiast's comment
ἐπιμόνως (apparently a corruption of ἐπιπόνως); against it is the fact
that σμυγερός does not occur elsewhere in tragedy, where μογερός is
the normal form. (See Jebb *ad loc.*) There is no certain instance of
σμυγερός before Apollonius, and the word is clearly a literary coinage
modeled on the Homeric ἐπισμυγερῶς. Such coinages are especially
typical of poets of the Hellenistic age.

§11. Xenophon *Historia Graeca* 5.2.6

οἰομένων δὲ ἀποθανεῖσθαι τῶν †ἀργυρολογιζόντων† καὶ τῶν
τοῦ δήμου προστατῶν, διεπράξατο ὁ πατὴρ παρὰ τοῦ Ἀγησι-
πόλιδος ἀσφάλειαν αὐτοῖς γενέσθαι ἀπαλλαττομένοις ἐκ τῆς
πόλεως, ἑξήκοντα οὖσι.

Stephanus' conjecture ἀργολιζόντων is necessary. ἀργυρολογίζω is a
vox nihili, but the cognates ἀργυρολογία, ἀργυρολόγος, ἀργυρολογέω
are of much commoner occurrence than ἀργολίζω ("take the part of
the Argives"), whence the error. For the corruption in various stages
compare *HG* 4.8.34 καὶ γὰρ ἀπεκτόνει τινὰς τῶν ἀργολιζόντων. The
MSS here give variously ἀργολιζόντων (D), ἀργολογιζόντων (BFMP),
ἀργυρολογιζόντων (CU). Corruption was perhaps facilitated by the
fact that ἠργυρολόγει occurs a little before (4.8.30).

§12. Plutarch *Moralia* 362A (*De Iside et Osiride* 28)

καὶ μέντοι Ἡρακλείτου τοῦ φυσικοῦ λέγοντος, "'Ἄιδης καὶ
Διόνυσος οὗτος ὅτε οὖν μαίνονται καὶ ληραίνουσιν," εἰς ταύτην
ὑπάγουσι τὴν δόξαν.

Clement of Alexandria (*Protrepticus* 2.34.5) quotes in full this fragment
of Heraclitus (15 Diels–Kranz); there we read in part ωὑτὸς δὲ Ἀίδης
καὶ Διόνυσος, ὅτεῳ μαίνονται καὶ ληναΐζουσιν, "Hades and Dionysus
are the same, in honor of whom they act mad and celebrate Lenaean
rites." Three distinct trivializations therefore in one sentence of Plutarch. Wyttenbach corrected οὗτος to ωὑτὸς and ὅτε οὖν to ὅτεῳ;
Bernardakis wrote ληναΐζουσιν for ληραίνουσιν. οὗτος and ὅτε οὖν are
mere slips due to the unfamiliar Ionic forms; in context they are meaningless. It is reasonable to assume—but not certain—that the corruptions happened within the MS tradition of Plutarch. ληραίνουσιν is

more difficult; μαίνονται καὶ ληραίνουσιν ("they act mad and rave") makes perfect sense. ληραίνουσιν may be either an accidental trivialization or a conscious conjecture made by someone who did not understand the meaning of ληναΐζουσιν (which, furthermore, being a rare word, may have first suffered a partial corruption). In other words, it is clear that Heraclitus wrote ληναΐζουσιν (compare frag. 14 ... βάκχοις, λήναις ...); whether Plutarch ⟨read in his immediate source and⟩ wrote ληναΐζουσιν or ληραίνουσιν is uncertain. Indeed, if Plutarch were quoting from memory, ληραίνουσιν could be nothing more than a very natural psychological *lapsus memoriae*. In cases such as this one, editors too readily assume that the corruption took place within the direct MS tradition of the writer who is quoting rather than in his source. It is instructive to reflect that, had Plutarch alone preserved this fragment, no one would have questioned the soundness of ληραίνουσιν, much less conjectured ληναΐζουσιν.

§13. Euripides *Phoenissae* 45–50

ὡς δ᾽ ἐπεζάρει
Σφὶγξ ἁρπαγαῖσι πόλιν ἐμός τ᾽ οὐκ ἦν πόσις,
Κρέων ἀδελφὸς τἀμὰ κηρύσσει λέχη,
ὅστις σοφῆς αἴνιγμα παρθένου μάθοι,
τούτῳ ξυνάψειν λέκτρα. τυγχάνει δέ πως
αἴνιγμ᾽ ἐμὸς παῖς Οἰδίπους Σφιγγὸς μαθών.

So read the MSS, and in the absence of further evidence there would be no adequate reason for questioning them. One might object stylistically to the repetition σοφῆς αἴνιγμα παρθένου ... αἴνιγμ᾽ ... Σφιγγὸς, but Euripides often repeats in close proximity the same word; compare μάθοι (48) ... μαθών (50). Such repetitions are characteristic of Greek epic and dramatic poets, and the objection is a "modern" one. Nevertheless, Euripides in fact did not write αἴνιγμ᾽ ... Σφιγγὸς. The scholiast remarks τινὲς γράφουσι "μούσας ἐμὸς παῖς," ὃ καὶ βέλτιον. Thus

16

there is evidence for an ancient variant μούσας ... Σφιγγὸς, which the scholiast correctly prefers and which editors have generally accepted. μοῦσα as an appellative in various senses is a favorite word of Euripides. One readily understands how the poetic, but obscure, expression μούσας ... Σφιγγὸς was replaced by αἴνιγμ' ... Σφιγγὸς; in origin αἴνιγμ' was probably a marginal or interlineal gloss, perhaps suggested by αἴνιγμα in verse 48. On the other hand, had Euripides written the perfectly clear αἴνιγμ' ... Σφιγγὸς, the presence of the somewhat singular and by no means perfectly synonymous variant μούσας is inexplicable. That is to say, αἴνιγμ' ... Σφιγγὸς could easily have arisen as an approximate paraphrase of μούσας ... Σφιγγὸς, but no one would have paraphrased an original αἴνιγμ' by μούσας.

§14. *Epinomis* 979D-E

ΚΛ. Ὦ ξένε, ὡς εἰκότως εἶπες ὅτι περὶ μεγάλων μεγάλα ἐπιχειρεῖς φράζειν.

ΑΘ. Οὐ γὰρ σμικρά, ὦ Κλεινία· τὸ δὲ χαλεπώτερον, ὅτι παντάπασι καὶ πάντως ἀληθῆ.

ΚΛ. Σφόδρα γε, ὦ ξένε· ἀλλ' ὅμως μὴ ἀποκάμῃς λέγων ὃ φῄς.

Solmsen, *CP* 56 (1961) 252–253, rightly called attention to the oddness of the Athenian's answer here: "... why should there be a correlation between the truth (or the degree of truth) of a subject and the difficulties inherent in an attempt to explain it?" Solmsen saw that the author must have written not ἀληθῆ, but ἀήθη. His parallel from *Laws* 891D–E (where the context is similar) is decisive:

ΚΛ. Εὖ λέγεις· ἀλλ' ὅπῃ, πειρῶ φράζειν.

ΑΘ. Ἔοικεν τοίνυν ἀηθεστέρων ἁπτέον εἶναι λόγων.

ΚΛ. Οὐκ ὀκνητέον, ὦ ξένε. μανθάνω γὰρ ...

ΑΘ. Λέγοιμ' ἄν, ὡς ἔοικεν, ἤδη σχεδὸν οὐκ εἰωθότα λόγον τινὰ τόνδε.

17

The same confusion occurs, as Solmsen notes, at *Euthydemus* 277D5, where B and W give ἀληθεῖς οἱ λόγοι, T and γρ. W correctly preserve ἀήθεις [for γρ.=γράφεται see below, sec. 26].

§15. Euripides *Orestes* 233–234

ἦ κἀπὶ γαίας ἁρμόσαι πόδας θέλεις,
χρόνιον ἴχνος θείς; μεταβολὴ πάντων γλυκύ.

In verse 234 P substitutes ἡδύ for γλυκύ. Meter proves γλυκύ to be the correct reading. ἡδύ illustrates two types of error: lapse of memory at the end of a verse (verses often being copied a line at a time) and unconscious substitution of the commoner synonym.

§16. Euripides *Electra* 1020–1024

κεῖνος δὲ παῖδα τὴν ἐμὴν Ἀχιλλέως
λέκτροισι πείσας ᾤχετ' ἐκ δόμων ἄγων
πρυμνοῦχον Αὖλιν, ἔνθ' ὑπερτείνας πύλας
λευκὴν διήμησ' Ἰφιγόνης παρηΐδα.

Tyrwhitt corrected πύλας in verse 1023 to πυρᾶς. The parallel that he cites from the *Iphigeneia in Tauris*, verses 24–27, is convincing:

καί μ' Ὀδυσσέως τέχναις
μητρὸς παρείλοντ' ἐπὶ γάμοις Ἀχιλλέως.
ἐλθοῦσα δ' Αὐλίδ' ἡ τάλαιν' ὑπὲρ πυρᾶς
μεταρσία ληφθεῖσ' ἐκαινόμην ξίφει.

One or more of the following factors could have caused the error: (1) πυρᾶς occurs at the end of a verse; (2) πύλη is a commoner word than πυρά; (3) a confusion of sound, λ and ρ both being liquids.

§17. Apollonius Rhodius *Argonautica* 1.234–235

αὐτὰρ ἐπεὶ δμώεσσιν ἐπαρτέα πάντ' ἐτέτυκτο
ὅσσα περ ἐντύνονται †ἐπαρτέα† ἔνδοθι νῆες.

ἐπαρτέα PE : ἐπαρτέες LASG

ἐπαρτέα in verse 235 is clearly an unconscious repetition of the adjective from verse 234, and the variant ἐπαρτέες is just as clearly a conscious—and clumsy—attempt to make sense of the passage. What did Apollonius actually write? There is no one word whose restoration is demanded by the context, and in errors of this sort the intruder need bear no resemblance to the ejected word(s). It is often, therefore, impossible to recover by conjecture the true reading. Nor, in fact, did anyone correct the text here; editors have either printed the unsatisfactory ἐπαρτέες or obelized †ἐπαρτέα† as corrupt. (Those editors who printed ἐπαρτέα between daggers acted correctly; the word was clearly unsound and should have been signalized as such.) The original lection has now been recovered from a papyrus: ἐπήρεες, "equipped" (see Fränkel's OCT of Apollonius, *praefatio critica*, p. vii). LSJ cite three instances of this adjective (Agatharchides frag. 83, Arrian *Anab.* 5.7.3, and Maximus Astrologus 415); two of these instances are nautical: Agatharchides uses it of πλοῖα and Arrian of a κελήτιον. The reading of the papyrus is quite convincing: (a) ἐπήρεες is appropriate in context; (b) it is perfectly clear how a word beginning ἐπηρ- could have been unconsciously replaced by ἐπαρτέα of the preceding line; (c) once the corruption to ἐπαρτέα had occurred, it is improbable that anyone would have recovered ἐπήρεες (apparently not a common word, at least in the classical and Alexandrian period) by conjecture. The papyrus has ἐπήρεες because that is what Apollonius wrote.

19

§18. Apollonius Rhodius *Argonautica* 1.721ff

721   αὐτὰρ ὅγ' ἀμφ' ὤμοισι, θεᾶς 'Ιτωνίδος ἔργον,
        δίπλακα πορφυρέην περονήσατο . . .

       .   .   .   .   .   .

727   δὴ γάρ τοι μέσση μὲν ἐρευθήεσσα τέτυκτο·
        ἄκρα δὲ πορφυρέη πάντη πέλεν, ἐν δ' ἄρ' ἑκάστῳ
        τέρματι δαίδαλα πολλὰ διακριδὸν εὖ ἐκέκαστο.

For ἐκέκαστο in verse 729 Ruhnken proposed ἐπέπαστο, which editors have rightly accepted. κέκασμαι, "be adorned, embellished," elsewhere is used with a dative of the means of embellishment; for example, Pindar *Ol.* 1.27 ἐλέφαντι ὦμον κεκαδμένον and, in Apollonius himself (4.1585), νεότητι κεκασμένα γυῖα. Here, therefore, we should have expected the construction ἕκαστον τέρμα δαιδάλοις πολλοῖς ἐκέκαστο. As parallels for πάσσω Ruhnken cited *Iliad* 3.125–127:

              ἡ δὲ μέγαν ἱστὸν ὕφαινε,
  δίπλακα πορφυρέην, πολέας δ' ἐνέπασσεν ἀέθλους,
  Τρώων θ' ἱπποδάμων καὶ 'Αχαιῶν χαλκοχιτώνων

and *Iliad* 22.440–441:

    ἀλλ' ἥ γ' ἱστὸν ὕφαινε μυχῷ δόμου ὑψηλοῖο
    δίπλακα πορφυρέην, ἐν δὲ θρόνα ποικίλ' ἔπασσε.

Fränkel further compares Nonnus *Dionysiaca* 28.5–6, a passage which should remove all doubt:

    ἀσπίδα χαλκείην πολυδαίδαλον. ἧς ἐνὶ κύκλῳ
    δαίδαλα πολλὰ πέπαστο.

The source of the error is clear: ἐκέκαστο was written by a copyist whose eye had caught the ἑκάστῳ of the preceding verse. Codex L has here the glosses ἐκεκόσμητο, ἐπέκειτο, which some regard as evidence for ἐπέπαστο. This cannot be pressed; had Apollonius written ἐκέκαστο, the meaning it would have to bear is clear from context. The glosses may very well be explanations of an already corrupt †ἐκέκαστο†, explanations determined by the apparent meaning of the word.

§19. Xenophon *Symposium* 3.7

τί γὰρ σύ, ἔφη, ὦ Κριτόβουλε, ἐπὶ τίνι μέγιστον φρονεῖς; Ἐπὶ κάλλει, ἔφη. Ἦ οὖν καὶ σύ, ἔφη ὁ Σωκράτης, ἕξεις λέγειν ὅτι τῷ σῷ κάλλει ἱκανὸς εἶ βελτίους ἡμᾶς ποιεῖν;

ὁ Σωκράτης Castalio : ὦ σώκρατες codd.

Castalio's correction is guaranteed by the context, from which it is clear that Socrates is asking the question. It is true that ὁ and ὦ would have been pronounced identically by a Byzantine Greek, but to explain the corruption as due to an error of sound is an oversimplification. The real cause of corruption here is the *psychological* factor; the copyist was unconsciously influenced to write ὦ σώκρατες because the preceding καὶ σύ had prepared him to expect a vocative. The collocation τί γὰρ σύ, ἔφη, ὦ Κριτόβουλε, still fresh in the copyist's mind, of course also helped to facilitate corruption. One hears constantly—and not unreasonably—of errors due to visual confusion of letters and to aural confusion of sounds. But a more elusive corrupter than either the copyist's eye or his ear is his brain. What was the copyist thinking as he transcribed the text before him? His thoughts, which often would be quite detached from the context of the MS, his "stream of consciousness" with the infinite variety of mental associations implied by this term, seduced the scribe time and time again. (This is one very important reason why so often we cannot give an exact explanation of a particular corruption, even after the passage seems to have been correctly emended; for we can seldom know what the man who made the error of transcription was thinking at the time. A little reflection on the psychology of the copyist suffices to give the lie to those who refuse to accept conjectures, in themselves most convincing on grounds of language, context, and style, solely because it is no longer apparent how the conjecture, if correct, would have physically altered into the lection found in the MSS.) The majority of errors of sight and sound are at the same time psychological errors; the contrary does not follow. For errors of this sort, therefore, see the examples in this book, *passim* (note especially Fraenkel's comments on *Agamemnon* 1391, quoted below, sec. 58). I cite here a few more obvious ones.

§20. Eustathius 989.38

καὶ περὶ Σεμέλης δέ, ἣν καὶ εἰς ἄμπελόν τινες, ἧς ὁ ἄνεμος κατα-
σείει μέλη, ἐν τοῖς κατὰ τὴν Θεογονίαν ἀλληγοροῦσιν, ὡς καὶ
τὸν Διόνυσον εἰς οἶνον . . .

  ἄνεμος West : οἶνος

ἄνεμος is confirmed by a parallel passage in an allegorical commentary to the *Theogony* composed by a certain Ioannes Diaconus Galenus (edited by H. Flach, *Glossen und Scholien zur hesiodischen Theogonie*, Leipzig 1876). (I owe my knowledge of both these passages to M. L. West's edition of Hesiod's *Theogony* [Oxford 1966] pp. 70–71.) Whether Eustathius is borrowing directly from Diaconus or whether they both derive from a common source is uncertain; the relevant passage (p. 359.8 Flach) is as follows: Σεμέλη δὲ ἡ ἄμπελος λέγεται ὡς σειόμενα ὑπ' ἀνέμων ἔχουσα τὰ μέλη. In this piece of etymological allegorism Σεμέλη is equated with the vine and her name is derived from σείω–μέλη. Clearly, vines are rustled by the wind, not wine, and ἄνεμος must be read in Eustathius. οἶνος is a patent psychological error: first, Semele, the mother of the god of wine, is mentioned; then the vine, the source of wine; and finally Dionysus, the very incarnation of wine. One readily understands how, in such a context, a scribe might unconsciously write οἶνος for ἄνεμος. Indeed, it is by no means certain that Eustathius found the error already present in his source. The archbishop of Thessalonica could easily have made the slip himself in his own autograph MS. It is very doubtful that, in the case of a work of

22

any length, the author ever succeeds in producing a manuscript completely free of accidental slips (which may or may not be detected and corrected before copies begin to be made of the autograph).

§21. Plutarch *Moralia* 433B (*De Defectu Oraculorum* 41)

περὶ δὲ τοῦ Κύδνου καὶ τῆς ἱερᾶς τοῦ Ἀπόλλωνος ἐν Ταρσῷ μα-
χαίρας, ὦ φίλε Δημήτριε, σοῦ λέγοντος ἠκούομεν, ὡς <οὔθ᾽> ὁ
Κύδνος [μ]ἄλλον ἐκκαθαίρει σίδηρον <ἢ> ἐκεῖνον οὔθ᾽ ὕδωρ
ἄλλο τὴν μάχαιραν ἢ ἐκεῖνο.

κύδνου E : κυάμου   <οὔθ᾽> Emperius   ἄλλον Emperius : μᾶλλον
<ἢ> Emperius

All the MSS except E give κυάμου instead of the clearly correct river-name Κύδνου (in E, of course, κύδνου represents an easy conjectural restoration, not genuine MS tradition). The corruption is simple enough in uncial script (ΚΥΔΝΟΥ:ΚΥΑΜΟΥ), the more familiar word, as so often, supplanting the rarer one. In this instance, however, we can be more specific; the copyist was psychologically conditioned to write κυάμου because in the immediately preceding sentence he had just written

ἀλλὰ γὰρ ἄλλοις οἰκεῖα καὶ πρόσφορα, καθάπερ τῆς μὲν πορ-
φύρας ὁ κύαμος τῆς δὲ κόκκου τὸ νίτρον δοκεῖ τὴν βαφὴν
ἄγειν (?) μεμιγμένον . . .

Moreover, in this prior sentence Paton regarded κύαμος as corrupt and conjectured κύανος. In connection with this it should be noted that the corruption below of κύδνου to κυάμου presupposes the lection κύαμος, not κύανος, here. This in itself does not refute the conjecture κύανος (a false one, in my judgment); what it does do is demonstrate that κύαμος, if unsound, must be a very old, pre-archetypal, corruption.

23

§22. Euripides *Iphigeneia Aulidensis* 382–384

τίς ἀδικεῖ σε; τοῦ κέχρησαι; χρηστὰ λέκτρ' ἐρᾷς λαβεῖν;
οὐκ ἔχοιμ' ἄν σοι παρασχεῖν· ὧν γὰρ ἐκτήσω, κακῶς
ἦρχες. εἶτ' ἐγὼ δίκην δῶ σῶν κακῶν, ὁ μὴ σφαλείς;

δῶ σῶν Dawes : δώσω

Agamemnon is addressing Menelaus in this speech. The question in verse 384 has a future reference; hence the copyist was psychologically disposed to expect a future tense and unwittingly wrote δώσω. Dawes's δῶ σῶν is convincing; the deliberative subjunctive is natural here and σῶν, providing as it does the desired contrast to ἐγώ, is a decided improvement.

§23. Xenophon *Respublica Lacedaemoniorum* 3.5

ἐκείνων γοῦν ἧττον μὲν ἂν φωνὴν ἀκούσαις ἢ τῶν λιθίνων, ἧττον
δ' ἂν ὄμματα μεταστρέψαις ἢ τῶν χαλκῶν, αἰδημονεστέρους δ'
ἂν αὐτοὺς ἡγήσαιο καὶ αὐτῶν τῶν ἐν τοῖς θαλάμοις παρθένων.

Xenophon is here lauding the virtues of Spartan youths: "You would be more likely," he assures us, "to hear stone statues idly talking than these young laconics; sooner could you induce bronze images to cast round inquisitive glances; *they* keep their eyes directed straight in front of them. Why, you would have to regard them as more modest than the very virgins in their rooms." So runs the passage in the MSS and I doubt that anyone would have questioned it, had not Pseudo-Longinus cited and criticized it in the *De Sublimitate* (4.4). Even Xenophon and Plato, he says, sometimes διὰ τὰ οὕτως μικροχαρῆ forget themselves; he then quotes the section given above as a specimen of extravagant writing. The quotation ends with the phrase τῶν ἐν τοῖς ὀφθαλμοῖς παρθένων; that this is no slip is shown by the next sentence: Ἀμφικράτει καὶ οὐ Ξενοφῶντι ἔπρεπε τὰς ἐν τοῖς ὀφθαλμοῖς ἡμῶν κόρας λέγειν παρθένους αἰδήμονας· οἷον δέ, ῾Ηράκλεις, τὸ τὰς ἁπάντων ἐξῆς κόρας αἰσχυντηλὰς εἶναι πεπεῖσθαι, ὅπου φασὶν ⟨ἐν?⟩ οὐδενὶ οὕτως ἐνσημαίνεσθαι τήν τινων ἀναίδειαν ὡς ἐν τοῖς ὀφθαλμοῖς . . . ("Longinus" goes on to cite a sentence from Timaeus the historian to illustrate how this writer has even capped the stylistic frigidity of Xenophon's phrase; the quotation goes as follows: ὃ τίς ἂν ἐποίησεν ἐν ὀφθαλμοῖς κόρας, μὴ πόρνας ἔχων;) "Longinus" is perhaps a bit hypercritical here. Xenophon's hyperbole consists merely in stating that Spartan youths are more silent than that which has to be silent— stone; their eyes are more immobile than eyes which cannot move— those in bronze images; and, finally, they are more modest than those virgins who cannot violate their virginity—αἱ ἐν τοῖς ὀφθαλμοῖς παρθένοι. This is flamboyant writing indeed, and "Longinus" rightly disapproves of it. When one understands correctly the point of Xenophon's threefold hyperbole, it becomes clear that the sense of the passage demands τῶν ἐν ὀφθαλμοῖς παρθένων to correspond to τῶν λιθίνων and τῶν χαλκῶν. The correct reading ὀφθαλμοῖς has been preserved not only by "Longinus" but also by Stobaeus (*Flor.* vol. 4, p. 145 Hense). Further confirmation is to be found in the medical writer Aretaeus of Cappadocia (second century A.D.), who uses the expression ἡ ἐν τοῖσι ὀφθαλμοῖσι παρθένος (p. 46.2–3 Hude) in an independent context.

θαλάμοις in the Xenophon MSS is a psychological error caused by a misunderstanding of the meaning of παρθένων here; recall that θάλαμος is very frequently used specifically of the women's quarters in a Greek house. Under such conditions, a swift reader could easily take ὀφθαλμοῖς as θαλάμοις; the two words are similar enough in appearance to cause the slip. For comparable confusions, see *h. Ven.* 189 βιοθάλμιος (corrupted to βιοφθάλμιος in some MSS) and Pindar *Olympian* 7.11 ζωθάλμιος (corrupted to ζωοφθάλμιος in the ζ family). (Of course, we cannot exclude the possibility that θαλάμοις is a conscious conjecture made by someone who did not understand the passage.) I mention as a curiosity the fact that θαλάμη is the technical anatomical term in Greek for the *optic thalamus* and is also used of the *eye socket*. It is unlikely in the extreme that mental associations between ὀφθαλμός and θαλάμη influenced the corruption to θαλάμοις; the average Greek, ancient or Byzantine, no more knew this meaning of θαλάμη than an average layman knows what the optic thalamus is.

Finally, on the basis of the same two citations in "Longinus" and Stobaeus, editors generally print [μετα]στρέψαις in Xenophon; μετα could have arisen by dittography with the preceding ὄμματα.

§24. Galen *De Usu Partium* 15.3 (4.222 Kühn = 2.345.12-14 Helmreich)

ἐπεὶ δὲ καὶ ἡ κύστις ἐτέτακτο πλησίον, ἕτερον οὐκ ἦν ἄμεινον ἐκκρίσεως οὔρων ἐργάζεσθαι πόρον †ἄλλον† ἢ συγχρήσασθαι τῷ τοῦ σπέρματος.

ἄλλον : ἀλλ' Helmreich

ἄλλον is redundant here after ἕτερον; Helmreich's conjecture misuses the phrase ἀλλ' ἤ. Galen wrote μᾶλλον, which the copyist, conditioned by the presence of ἕτερον, misread as ἄλλον. The fact that the word preceding μᾶλλον ends in -N facilitated the slip. Editors of Galen must blush for failing to notice that the physician Oribasius (the intimate friend of Julian the Apostate), who quotes this passage verbatim (3. [= CMG 6.2.1] 41.15–17 Raeder), preserves the correct reading μᾶλλον. [See my *Lectiones Galenicae* in *Rh. Mus.* 108 (1965) 70.]

§25. St. Basil *In Hexaemeron* 3.2 (Migne, PG 29.55C-56A)

πρῶτον μὲν οὖν ἀναλαβόντες ζητῶμεν πῶς ὁ θεὸς διαλέγεται. Ἆρα τὸν ἡμέτερον τρόπον, πρότερον μὲν ὁ ἀπὸ τῶν πραγμάτων τύπος ἐγγίνεται τῇ νοήσει, ἔπειτα μετὰ τὸ φαντασθῆναι, ἀπὸ τῶν ὑποκειμένων τὰς οἰκείας καὶ προσφυεῖς ἑκάστου σημασίας

ἐκλεγόμενος ἐξαγγέλλει; εἶτα τῇ ὑπηρεσίᾳ τῶν φωνητικῶν
ὀργάνων παραδοὺς τὰ νοηθέντα, οὕτω διὰ τῆς τοῦ ἀέρος τυπώ-
σεως, κατὰ τὴν ἔναρθρον τῆς φωνῆς κίνησιν, ἐν τῷ κρυπτῷ νόημα
σαφηνίζει;

This is the text as it appears in the printed editions. An editor could
have improved it in three places, had he availed himself of the still
accessible means. Meletius Monachus, a Byzantine doxographer of the
ninth century (?), quotes the passage from πρότερον to the end (PG
64.1105B–C). For φαντασθῆναι he has φαντασιωθῆναι, which is also
the reading of several Basilian MSS. As the rarer verb, it is a *lectio
difficilior* and should be received into the text here. φαντάζεσθαι,
though it may mean "to form an image," "to imagine," had also
developed a pejorative sense, "to imagine," meaning "to suppose in-
correctly." So Basil uses it above, p. 4A: οὐρανοῦ γὰρ καὶ γῆς ποίησις
παραδίδοσθαι μέλλει, οὐκ αὐτομάτως συνενεχθεῖσα, ὥς τινες ἐφαν-
τάσθησαν, παρὰ δὲ τοῦ θεοῦ τὴν αἰτίαν λαβοῦσα. φαντασιοῦσθαι, on
the other hand, was a technical term of later Greek cognitive theory;
Basil uses it below, 61C: . . . δεδιδαγμένοι παρὰ τῆς γραφῆς, μηδὲν
ἐπιτρέπειν ἡμῶν τῷ νῷ πέρα τῶν συγκεχωρημένων φαντασιοῦσθαι.

In place of παραδοὺς the MSS of Meletius are divided between
παραδιδοὺς and διαδιδοὺς; comparison with our passage of Basil confirms παραδιδοὺς for Meletius. In Basil we should correct to παρα⟨δι⟩-
δοὺς; the present is better and the haplography an easy corruption. A
certain Eustathius, who, about A.D. 400, made a still extant Latin translation of Basil's *In Hexaemeron*, also seems to have read the present: "et
post hoc ministeriis vocalium officiorum [= ὀργάνων] cogitata *mani-
festantes* . . ." (p. 32.21–22 Amand de Mendieta-Rudberg).

Finally, ἐν τῷ κρυπτῷ νόημα σαφηνίζει should mean something like
"in the secret place (*or*: in secret) he explains his thought." In context
this is nonsense; the restoration of an article which Meletius has preserved sets everything right: ⟨τὸ⟩ ἐν τῷ κρυπτῷ νόημα σαφηνίζει. For
the meaning of this expression, compare below, 56C, where Basil
speaks of τῶν ἐν καρδίᾳ νοημάτων. The opening words of Basil's
homily *in illud attende tibi ipsi* (PG 31.197C–D) should also be com-

pared, particularly the expression ὥσπερ ἔκ τινων ταμιείων, τῶν τῆς καρδίας κρυπτῶν. These phrases derive from the New Testament; compare especially Matthew 6.6: σὺ δέ, ὅταν προσεύχῃ, εἴσελθε εἰς τὸ ταμιεῖόν σου, καὶ κλείσας τὴν θύραν σου πρόσευξαι τῷ πατρί σου τῷ ἐν τῷ κρυπτῷ· καὶ ὁ πατήρ σου ὁ βλέπων ἐν τῷ κρυπτῷ ἀποδώσει σοι. See also Matthew 6.4, 6.18; 1 Cor. 14.25, and in the LXX, Prov. 20.27. [The above discussion, in a slightly altered form, was first published in *HSCP* 67 (1963) 278–279.]

§26. Euripides *Phoenissae* 1335–1336

— ὦ τάλας ἐγώ, τίν᾽ εἴπω μῦθον ἢ τίνας λόγους;
— οἰχόμεσθ᾽· οὐκ εὐπροσώποις φροιμίοις ἄρχῃ λόγου.

Verse 1335 will make sense as it stands, but there is no doubt that Porson's γόους is an improvement. λόγους is a slip caused by λόγου of verse 1336 (a slip for which the copyist was psychologically conditioned by τίν᾽ εἴπω μῦθον). In verse 1309 above, παύσω τοὺς παρεστῶτας γόους, the same corruption to the commoner word λόγους happened in codex V. There is another example in the *Orestes*, verses 1022–1024:

οὐ σῖγ᾽ ἀφεῖσα τοὺς γυναικείους γόους
στέρξεις τὰ κρανθέντ᾽; οἰκτρὰ μὲν τάδ᾽, ἀλλ᾽ ὅμως
[φέρειν σ᾽ ἀνάγκη τὰς παρεστώσας τύχας].

Here γόους has been preserved only as a "γράφεται," that is a variant, in M and B; all the MSS give λόγους in the text. This passage also illustrates a different kind of error, *interpolation*. The scholiast did not have verse 1024 in his copy, for he comments λείπει τὸ δεῖ φέρειν. τινὲς δὲ γράφουσιν οἰκτρὰ μὲν ἀλλ᾽ ὅμως φέρε. The verse was added by someone who did not understand this elliptical usage of ἀλλ᾽ ὅμως (see LSJ s.v. ὅμως I); examples of it in Euripides may be seen at *Electra* 753, *Hecuba* 843, and *IA* 904. Paley in his commentary observes "The next verse [1024] is with very good reason regarded by Kirchhoff as an

28

interpolation. The dialogue commences, as usual, with twice the number of verses spoken subsequently." (That is, Electra speaks four verses, 1018–1021, then there follows an exchange between her and Orestes in which each speaks two lines at a time. The offending verse, 1024, allots three lines to Orestes and destroys the symmetry.) Compare *Bacchae* 1027–1028:

> ὥς σε στενάζω, δοῦλος ὢν μέν, ἀλλ᾽ ὅμως
> [χρηστοῖσι δούλοις συμφορὰ τὰ δεσποτῶν].

Dobree deleted verse 1028, which someone "borrowed" from *Medea* 54–55:

> χρηστοῖσι δούλοις ξυμφορὰ τὰ δεσποτῶν
> κακῶς πίτνοντα, καὶ φρενῶν ἀνθάπτεται.

These two verses clearly belong together; the first verse alone (= "masters' concerns are a misfortune to good slaves") is nonsense. Dodds, in his edition of the *Bacchae*, comments "Such interpolations are late, and should not be attributed to actors. Cf. *Or.* 1023, where the same idiom gave rise (a) to a similar interpolation which appears in all MSS but is unknown to the scholiasts, (b) to an unmetrical (and therefore late) emendation quoted in a scholion." (ἀλλ᾽ ὅμως occurs also at *HF* 1365 and *Tr.* 366; in the first instance Nauck deleted verse 1366, in the second Wecklein deleted verse 367.)

§27

It is convenient to give here some further examples of interpolations. Let it be clearly understood that there is only one feature common to all interpolations: the fact that they are all extraneous additions to a genuine text. The origin and causes of specific interpolations may be quite diverse, and one should beware of regarding "interpolation" as a single definite category of error. Some interpolations are intentional, others accidental. The motives of deliberate interpolators range from the patriotic or religious to the frivolous. The ancients themselves were aware of the practice, and antiquity had its famous controversies. The verses on Salamis in the Homeric Catalogue of Ships (*Iliad* 2.557–558) are a well-known example:

> Αἴας δ' ἐκ Σαλαμῖνος ἄγεν δυοκαίδεκα νῆας,
> στῆσε δ' ἄγων ἵν' Ἀθηναίων ἵσταντο φάλαγγες.

A certain Dieuchidas of Megara and others accused Solon (or Pisistratus) of adding verse 558 to give support to Athens' claim to Salamis in her dispute with Megara.

Again, Pausanias (9.31.4) tells us the following:

> Βοιωτῶν δὲ οἱ περὶ τὸν Ἑλικῶνα οἰκοῦντες παρειλημμένα δόξῃ λέγουσιν ὡς ἄλλο Ἡσίοδος ποιήσειεν οὐδὲν ἢ τὰ Ἔργα· καὶ τούτων δὲ τὸ ἐς τὰς Μούσας ἀφαιροῦσι προοίμιον, ἀρχὴν τῆς ποιήσεως εἶναι τὸ ἐς τὰς Ἔριδας λέγοντες· καί μοι μόλυβδον ἐδείκνυσαν, ἔνθα ἡ πηγή, τὰ πολλὰ ὑπὸ τοῦ χρόνου λελυμασμένον· ἐγγέγραπται δὲ αὐτῷ τὰ Ἔργα.

The Boeotians, therefore, who lived around Helicon maintained that the proemium to the *Erga* (verses 1–10) was an interpolation. (For a discussion of this question see Sinclair's commentary, verses 1–10.)

Most scholars today regard Thucydides 3.84 as an interpolated chapter; if it is, it is a good specimen of deliberate and competent *imitation*. The arguments against its genuineness are well stated by Gomme in his *Commentary to Thucydides*. The interpolation of a single verse in the first Epistle of St. John (chapter 5, verse 7)—the famous "Three Heavenly Witnesses" verse—was responsible for a whole chapter in the history of scholarship. In the list of those who condemned the verse may be seen the names of Erasmus, Newton, Bentley, Gibbon, and Porson. Still more famous and still debated is the passage in Josephus (*Antiquitates Iudaicae* 17.63–64) about Jesus Christ, the so-called *Testimonium Flavianum*. For an example of whimsical interpolation, see Simias' *technopaegnium*, "Axe" (frag. 25 Powell=*AP* 15.22). This poem is shaped like an axe—but lacks a handle. Someone therefore interpolated a longish verse (fashioned in part from another *technopaegnium* of Simias, "Egg") to supply the axe handle! In the *Agricola* of Tacitus, chapter 24, Ireland is described as follows: *solum caelumque et ingenia cultusque hominum haud multum a Britannia differunt in melius.* Wex deleted the awkward words *in melius*. Gudeman notes in his commentary "*In melius* is, I am convinced, nothing more than a marginal or interlinear gloss of some patriotic Irish scribe—such are known to have been engaged in German scriptoria—which subsequently intruded into the text."

§28. Plutarch *Moralia* 431E-F (*De Defectu Oraculorum* 39)

διὰ τί τὰς ἐν τοῖς σώμασι ψυχὰς ἐκείνης τῆς δυνάμεως ἀποστεροῦμεν, ᾗ τὰ μέλλοντα καὶ προγιγνώσκειν πεφύκασι καὶ προδηλοῦν οἱ δαίμονες; οὔτε γὰρ δύναμιν οὔτε μέρος οὐδὲν ἐπιγίγνεσθαι ταῖς ψυχαῖς, ὅταν ἀπολίπωσι τὸ σῶμα, μὴ κεκτημέναις πρότερον εἰκός ἐστιν· ἀλλ' ἀεὶ μὲν ἔχειν, ἔχειν δὲ φαυλότερα τῷ σώματι μεμιγμένας, καὶ τὰ μὲν ὅλως ἄδηλα καὶ κεκρυμμένα τὰ δ' ἀσθενῆ καὶ ἀμαυρὰ καὶ τοῖς δι' ὀμίχλης ὁρῶσιν ἢ κινουμένοις ἐν ὑγρῷ παραπλησίως δύσεργα καὶ βραδέα καὶ πολλὴν ποθοῦντα θεραπείαν τοῦ οἰκείου καὶ ἀνάληψιν ἀφαίρεσιν δὲ καὶ κάθαρσιν τοῦ †κλέπτοντος.†

†κλέπτοντος† is clearly corrupt; Emperius (*Opuscula Philol. et Hist.*, p. 330) suggested καλύπτοντος, which restores sense and is generally accepted. (Though κρύπτοντος, which Emperius proposed as an alternate solution, is also possible; compare above, τὰ μὲν ὅλως ἄδηλα καὶ κεκρυμμένα.) Codex J (= Ambros. 881) has the following reading:

. . . καὶ κάθαρσιν τοῦ κωλύοντος ὅτι ἡ ψυχὴ καὶ συνδεδεμένη τῷ σώματι τὴν προγνωστικὴν ἔχει δύναμιν ἐκτυφλοῦται δὲ διὰ τὴν πρὸς τὸ γεῶδες ἀνάκρασιν τοῦ σώματος.

This is an interesting example of a scribe at work. There is no doubt that the copyist who wrote these words found κλέπτοντος in his exemplar; realizing that this verb in context was nonsense, he wrote by conjecture κωλύοντος in an attempt to set things right. Correctly

understanding that κωλύοντος alone was obscure, he thereupon interpolated the explanatory words ὅτι ἡ ψυχὴ . . . τοῦ σώματος. It should
be understood that no fraud was intended by such an interpolation; a
reverence for the exact preservation of an author's *ipsissima verba* is in
general a modern virtue. ["Distinction could be made of times and
texts; certainly in late and Byzantine times some texts—say Homer or
Plato—were copied with great fidelity, whereas others—say those of
Babrius or Aesop—were modified almost at will. Many of the variants
in the text of the New Testament arose before these writings became
canonical." B.E.]

§29. Euripides *Troiades* 551–555

> ἐγὼ δὲ τὰν ὀρεστέραν
> τότ᾽ ἀμφὶ μέλαθρα παρθένον
> Διὸς κόραν ["Αρτεμιν] ἐμελπόμαν
> χοροῖσι . . .

"Αρτεμιν interrupts the meter; it is nothing but an explanatory gloss
of ὀρεστέραν . . . παρθένον Διὸς κόραν which accidentally crept into
the text. Seidler correctly deleted it. The same error occurs in verse 825
of this play:

> μάταν ἄρ᾽, ὦ χρυσέαις ἐν οἰνοχόαις ἁβρὰ βαίνων,
>   Λαομεδόντιε παῖ,
> Ζηνὸς ἔχεις κυλίκων πλήρωμα, καλλίσταν λατρείαν·
> ἁ δέ σε γειναμένα [Τροία] πυρὶ δαίεται.

Musgrave made the deletion of Τροία.

§30. Euripides *Hecuba* 1085–1087

> ὦ τλῆμον, ὥς σοι δύσφορ᾽ εἴργασται κακά·
> δράσαντι δ᾽ αἰσχρὰ δεινὰ τἀπιτίμια.
> [δαίμων ἔδωκεν ὅστις ἐστί σοι βαρύς.]

Hermann excised verse 1087 as an interpolation which someone repeated from verses 722–723 of this play:

> ὦ τλῆμον, ὥς σε πολυπονωτάτην βροτῶν
> δαίμων ἔθηκεν ὅστις ἐστί σοι βαρύς.

Hermann's solution is surely correct. Verse 1086 alone is much more effective; the addition of verse 1087 produces an awkward and trite sentence. Furthermore these verses correspond to verses 1107–1108, where the chorus is allotted *two*, not three, lines. The alternation ἔθηκεν/ἔδωκεν is another indication that something is wrong at verse 1087. Only ἔθηκεν will make sense at verse 723 and is certainly the original verb: ἔδωκεν is a conscious adjustment of the interpolator. Even in verse 1087 a sense of sorts could be extracted from ἔθηκεν and the scribe of L actually writes ἔθηκεν—obviously "correcting" ἔδωκεν on the basis of verse 723 which he recalled. The interpolation of borrowed verses is common in Greek tragedy; for another example see the discussion of *Bacchae* 1027–1028, above, sec. 26.

§31. Sophocles *Trachiniae* 82–85

> ἐν οὖν ῥοπῇ τοιᾷδε κειμένῳ, τέκνον,
> οὐκ εἶ ξυνέρξων, ἡνίκ᾽ ἢ σεσώμεθα
> [ἢ πίπτομεν σου πατρὸς ἐξολωλότος]
> κείνου βίον σώσαντος, ἢ οἰχόμεσθ᾽ ἅμα;

Verses 84 and 85 obviously cannot both be retained in this passage, and it was Bentley who first understood the corruption: the two verses are doublets. Verse 85 is stylistically better, and Bentley rightly deleted verse 84. It has not been observed that ἐξολωλότος furnishes strong support to the correctness of this deletion; ἐξόλλυμι occurs nowhere else in Sophocles nor is it found in Aeschylus. In other words, ἐξόλλυμι does not seem to have been used in high tragic diction (its occurrence several times in Euripides, whose diction tended to become less elevated than that of Aeschylus and Sophocles, does not gainsay this;

compare below, sec. 47). Rather the verb belongs to the vocabulary of prose and comedy. The usual tragic verb was ὄλλυμι; see my "An Unnoticed Greek Tragic Fragment" in *Rh. Mus.* 109 (1966) 185-186. Whether verse 84 is an "actors' interpolation" or is to be explained in some other way, it does not belong to this passage.

A certain example of a conflated text occurs in the *Andromache* of Euripides, verses 3-7:

> Πριάμου τύραννον ἑστίαν ἀφικόμην
> δάμαρ δοθεῖσα παιδοποιὸς Ἕκτορι,
> ζηλωτὸς ἔν γε τῷ πρὶν Ἀνδρομάχη χρόνῳ,
> νῦν δ᾽, εἴ τις ἄλλη, δυστυχεστάτη γυνή·
> [ἐμοῦ πέφυκεν ἢ γενήσεταί ποτε]

εἴ τις : οὔτις V (corr. V²) Haun. *l*

Verses 6 and 7, as they stand, are a conflation of several ways of expressing the same thought: (a) "I, if any woman, am most unlucky"; (b) "no other woman is more unlucky than I"; (c) "no other woman than I is the most unlucky." The variant οὔτις for εἴ τις is probably nothing but a stopgap conjecture, made in an attempt to patch up the sense and grammar, after verse 7 had been interpolated. Dramatic style argues strongly for deletion; what is wanted is a concise contrast to verse 5. δυστυχεστάτη γυνή responds neatly to ζηλωτὸς and νῦν δ᾽ contrasts with ἔν γε τῷ πρὶν . . . χρόνῳ; the next verse destroys the balance and is superfluous. εἴ τις ἄλλη (*si quis alia*) is quite idiomatic; the editors compare Sophocles *Trachiniae* 7-8: νυμφείων ὄκνον / ἄλγιστον ἔσχον, εἴ τις Αἰτωλὶς γυνή. In this case we are fortunate in having external evidence which confirms the deletion (first suggested by Valckenaer). *P. Oxy.* 449 (third century A.D.) contains fragments of verses 5-48 of the *Andromache*; it omits verse 7. Furthermore, the scholiast states explicitly that this verse was interpolated by actors: ἐμοῦ πέφυκεν ἢ γενήσεταί ποτε: οἱ ὑποκριταὶ τὸν ἴαμβον προσέθηκαν ὑπονοήσαντες εἶναι τὴν γραφὴν "δὴ τίς," ἵν᾽ ᾖ οὕτως "νῦν δὴ τίς ἄλλη" καὶ ἀντὶ τοῦ συγκριτικοῦ τὸ δυστυχεστάτη φησίν.

§32. Euripides *Helen* 255-260

255   φίλαι γυναῖκες, τίνι πότμῳ συνεζύγην;
       ἆρ' ἡ τεκοῦσά μ' ἔτεκεν ἀνθρώποις τέρας;
       [γυνὴ γὰρ οὔθ' Ἑλληνὶς οὔτε βάρβαρος
       τεῦχος νεοσσῶν λευκὸν ἐκλοχεύεται,
       ἐν ᾧ με Λήδαν φασὶν ἐκ Διὸς τεκεῖν.]
260   τέρας γὰρ ὁ βίος καὶ τὰ πράγματ' ἐστί μου.

In this passage Helen is lamenting to the chorus of Greek women. Verses 257–259 were deleted, apparently independently, by Wieland and Badham, and are now usually regarded as an interpolation. There seems to be here another example of doublets in the text; the question asked in verse 256 is answered twice, first by verses 257–259, then by verse 260. The repeated γάρ (verses 257, 260) is stylistically indefensible. Here, however, the diction strongly argues for the genuineness of the lines. The uncommon verb ἐκλοχεύω occurs in only one other place in the extant remains of tragedy: in the *Ion*, verse 1458. τεῦχος, in various locutions, is a favorite word of Euripides, as may be seen by a glance at the concordance. The expression γυνὴ ... οὔθ' Ἑλληνὶς οὔτε βάρβαρος is paralleled in *Troiades* 477–478: οὐ (οὓς Stephanus) Τρῳὰς οὐδ' Ἑλληνὶς οὐδὲ βάρβαρος / γυνὴ τεκοῦσα ... (Here Hecuba is speaking, hence the traditional dichotomy into Greek and barbarian becomes a trichotomy: Trojan, Greek, barbarian.) A complex problem thus faces us. Earlier scholars have correctly seen that there is something amiss here, yet I believe that I have demonstrated that the deleted verses are in themselves quite Euripidean (nor has anyone offered a cogent reason for interpolation here). The solution is to be sought not in deletion, but in *transposition*:

255   φίλαι γυναῖκες, τίνι πότμῳ συνεζύγην;
257   γυνὴ γὰρ οὔθ' Ἑλληνὶς οὔτε βάρβαρος
258   τεῦχος νεοσσῶν λευκὸν ἐκλοχεύεται,
259   ἐν ᾧ με Λήδαν φασὶν ἐκ Διὸς τεκεῖν.
256   ἆρ' ἡ τεκοῦσά μ' ἔτεκεν ἀνθρώποις τέρας;
260   τέρας γὰρ ὁ βίος καὶ τὰ πράγματ' ἐστί μου.

With this order of verses there are two questions and two answers; each γάρ now becomes intelligible. The stylistic device of ending one line and beginning the next with the same word (τέρας) should also be observed. The cause of the error is easily explained. Verses 259 and 256 both end with words beginning τε; this caused the copyist's eye to skip accidentally from verse 259 to verse 260. Afterwards the error was noticed and the omitted verse 256 was added in the margin, whence in a later copy it was inserted into the text in the wrong position, presumably because the marginal sign indicating where the verse belonged was unclear or had vanished. Verses are often accidentally omitted; see the *apparatus criticus* of Murray's OCT of Euripides at *Orestes* 38, where he comments ". . . omisit tum in ima pagina restituit P" and at *Orestes* 89: "in textu omissum in margine add. M." It is unnecessary to multiply examples.

Marginal confusions also occur frequently in MSS; see Euripides *Phoenissae* 1072–1076:

> ὦ φίλτατ', οὔ που ξυμφορὰν ἥκεις φέρων
> Ἐτεοκλέους θανόντος, οὗ παρ' ἀσπίδα
> βέβηκας αἰεὶ πολεμίων εἴργων βέλη;
> [τί μοί ποθ' ἥκεις καινὸν ἀγγελῶν ἔπος;]
> τέθνηκεν ἢ ζῇ παῖς ἐμός; σήμαινέ μοι.

Valckenaer correctly deleted verse 1075 and supported his deletion by a scholium found in B: ἐν τοῖς πολλοῖς ἀντιγράφοις οὐ φέρεται οὗτος ὁ στίχος. This identical scholium is found also in V, where, however, it is referred to verse 1069, a verse which is certainly genuine; the learned marginal comment was simply misplaced.

§33. Euripides *Hecuba* 243–252

> — ἔγνω δέ σ' Ἑλένη καὶ μόνη κατεῖπ' ἐμοί;
> — μεμνήμεθ' ἐς κίνδυνον ἐλθόντες μέγαν.
> — ἦψω δὲ γονάτων τῶν ἐμῶν ταπεινὸς ὤν;
> — ὥστ' ἐνθανεῖν γε σοῖς πέπλοισι χεῖρ' ἐμήν.

247 — ἔσωσα δῆτά σ' ἐξέπεμψά τε χθονός;
248 — ὥστ' εἰσορᾶν γε φέγγος ἡλίου τόδε.
249 — τί δῆτ' ἔλεξας δοῦλος ὢν ἐμὸς τότε;
250 — πολλῶν λόγων εὕρημαθ', ὥστε μὴ θανεῖν.
— οὔκουν κακύνῃ τοῖσδε τοῖς βουλεύμασιν,
ὃς ἐξ ἐμοῦ μὲν ἔπαθες οἷα φῂς παθεῖν κτλ.

In this confrontation between Hecuba and Odysseus the verses are so collocated in the oldest and best MSS and Murray so prints them. The *"Byzantini,"* i.e. the *codices recentiores,* transpose 249–250 before 247–248 and this collocation has been accepted by Porson and others; Wecklein excised verses 249–250. There can be no doubt that the transposed order presents a much smoother logical sequence. Why then does Murray retain the transmitted order? Presumably because they do not give an absolutely impossible sense and because he could see no reason why the order of the verses should have become disarranged. In themselves, neither of these considerations is ever an adequate justification for the retention of an unsatisfactory text. In this particular case, let us transpose the verses and the cause of the corruption will become clear:

245 — ἥψω δὲ γονάτων τῶν ἐμῶν ταπεινὸς ὤν;
246 — ὥστ' ἐνθανεῖν γε σοῖς πέπλοισι χεῖρ' ἐμήν.
249 — τί δῆτ' ἔλεξας δοῦλος ὢν ἐμὸς τότε;
250 — πολλῶν λόγων εὕρημαθ', ὥστε μὴ θανεῖν.
247 — ἔσωσα δῆτά σ' ἐξέπεμψά τε χθονός;
248 — ὥστ' εἰσορᾶν γε φέγγος ἡλίου τόδε.
251 — οὔκουν κακύνῃ κτλ.

The scribe wrote a verse at a time; when he had written verse 246 with its ὥστ' ἐνθανεῖν, his eye happened to catch ὥστε μὴ θανεῖν in verse 250. Confusing the two phrases, he inadvertently thought that he had already copied down through verse 250 and proceeded to copy verses 247–248, omitting verses 249–250. Once again, the error having been detected, the two omitted verses were added in the margin or at the bottom of the page and, in the next copy, replaced to the text proper in the wrong position. (For a lucid discussion of the problem of transposed verses, see W. V. Clausen in *AJP* 76 [1955] 47–49.)

§34. Xenophon *Symposium* 4.36–37

I   τύραννοι δ᾽ εἰσί τινες οἳ ὅλους μὲν οἴκους ἀναιροῦσιν,
     ἀθρόους δ᾽ ἀποκτείνουσι, πολλάκις δὲ καὶ ὅλας πόλεις χρη-
     μάτων ἕνεκα ἐξανδραποδίζονται. τούτους μὲν οὖν ἔγωγε
     καὶ πάνυ οἰκτίρω τῆς ἄγαν χαλεπῆς νόσου. ὅμοια γάρ μοι
5   δοκοῦσι πάσχειν ὥσπερ εἴ τις πολλὰ ἔχων καὶ πολλὰ ἐσ-
     θίων μηδέποτε ἐμπίμπλαιτο. ἐγὼ δὲ οὕτω μὲν πολλὰ ἔχω
     ὡς μόλις αὐτὰ καὶ [ἐγὼ ἂν] αὐτὸς εὑρίσκω.

     5. ἔχων : πίνων Schneider : ἔχοι Nitsche   6. ἔχω : ἔχων
ABGH¹H²Hᵃ   7. ἐγὼ del. Cobet   ἂν om. B

πολλὰ ἔχων, which should mean "having many possessions," is out of
place and superfluous; there is certainly some corruption here. Schneider's πίνων is reasonable but is open to the objection that the normal
Greek word order would be πολλὰ ἐσθίων καὶ πολλὰ πίνων; for
example, Xenophon in the very next sentence writes . . . μοι καὶ
ἐσθίοντι . . . καὶ πίνοντι . . . (Homer's ὁ πῖνε καὶ ἦσθε, so written for
metrical reasons, does not gainsay this.) Again, Nitsche's πολλὰ ἔχοι,
a mere makeshift, is damned by its imbalance and superfluity. The fact
is that the words πολλὰ ἔχων are unnecessary to the comparison; see
the similar comparison in this work, chapter 8.15: καὶ μὴν ἐν μὲν τῇ
τῆς μορφῆς χρήσει ἔνεστί τις καὶ κόρος, ὥστε ἅπερ καὶ πρὸς τὰ
σιτία διὰ πλησμονήν, ταῦτα ἀνάγκη καὶ πρὸς τὰ παιδικὰ πάσχειν. I
therefore conjecture that πολλὰ ἔχων is an interpolation and should be
deleted. The source of the error is not far to seek. For πολλὰ ἔχω in
line 6 there was a variant πολλὰ ἔχων, which is still preserved in part of
the extant MS tradition. In an ancestor of the archetype this variant
πολλὰ ἔχων was written in the margin, whence someone erroneously
"restored" it to the text before καὶ πολλὰ ἐσθίων, influenced possibly
by a misunderstanding of the intensive usage of καὶ here. (It is also
possible that καί is a stopgap inserted along with πολλὰ ἔχων.)
[Correction: I see from the *apparatus criticus* of Thalheim's Teubner
edition of Xenophon that the deletion [πολλὰ ἔχων καὶ] has already

been proposed by Lange. What his reasons for deleting the words were I do not know, but he should be credited with having been the first to make the suggestion.]

§35. Epicurus *Epistle to Herodotus* (= Diogenes Laertius 10.35-83)

This epistle contains a number of demonstrable interpolations and is an interesting specimen of the vagaries of copyists. The interpolations are in fact marginal scholia which have been incorporated into the text. Interruptions of the thought sequence, learned and exact cross-references to other works of Epicurus, and telltale words such as φησί and λέγει leave no doubt as to the nature of these intruders (which indeed Bailey, in his edition of Epicurus, prints separately at the bottom of the page under the heading *Scholia*). Compare the following examples:

> καὶ μὴν καὶ τῶν [τοῦτο καὶ ἐν τῇ πρώτῃ Περὶ φύσεως καὶ τῇ ιδ´ καὶ ιε´ καὶ τῇ Μεγάλῃ ἐπιτομῇ] σωμάτων τὰ μέν ἐστι συγκρίσεις, τὰ δ᾽ ἐξ ὧν αἱ συγκρίσεις πεποίηνται.

(Diogenes Laertius 10.40)

> κινοῦνταί τε συνεχῶς αἱ ἄτομοι [φησὶ δὲ ἐνδοτέρω καὶ ἰσοταχῶς αὐτὰς κινεῖσθαι τοῦ κενοῦ τὴν εἶξιν ὁμοίαν παρεχομένου καὶ τῇ κουφοτάτῃ καὶ τῇ βαρυτάτῃ.]

(Diogenes Laertius 10.43)

> . . . ἴδιόν τι σύμπτωμα περὶ ταῦτα πάλιν αὐτὸ τοῦτο ἐννοοῦντες, καθ᾽ ὃ χρόνον ὀνομάζομεν. [φησὶ δὲ τοῦτο καὶ ἐν τῇ δευτέρᾳ Περὶ φύσεως καὶ ἐν τῇ Μεγάλῃ ἐπιτομῇ.]

(Diogenes Laertius 10.73)

> . . . καὶ πάλιν διαλύεσθαι πάντα, τὰ μὲν θᾶττον, τὰ δὲ βραδύτερον, καὶ τὰ μὲν ὑπὸ τῶν τοιῶνδε, τὰ δὲ ὑπὸ τῶν τοιῶνδε τοῦτο πάσχοντα. [δῆλον οὖν ὡς καὶ φθαρτούς φησι τοὺς κόσμους,

μεταβαλλόντων τῶν μερῶν. καὶ ἐν ἄλλοις τὴν γῆν τῷ ἀέρι
ἐποχεῖσθαι.]

(Diogenes Laertius 10.73)

δῆλον οὖν ὡς καὶ retinet von der Muehll, lacuna post καὶ indicata.

For other interpolations in this letter see Diogenes Laertius 10.39, 44,
50, 66, 74; scholia have also been introduced into the text of Epicurus'
Epistle to Pythocles (*ap.* Diogenes Laertius 10.84–116); for example:

καὶ ὧδε τοὺς οἰκείους ἀλλήλοις τρόπους συνθεωρητέον, καὶ τὰς
ἅμα συγκυρήσεις τινῶν ὅτι οὐκ ἀδύνατον γίνεσθαι [ἐν δὲ τῇ ιβ'
Περὶ φύσεως ταῦτα λέγει καὶ πρός, ἥλιον ἐκλείπειν σελήνης
ἐπισκοτούσης, σελήνην δὲ τοῦ τῆς γῆς σκιάσματος, ἀλλὰ καὶ
κατ' ἀναχώρησιν. τοῦτο δὲ καὶ Διογένης ὁ 'Επικούρειος ἐν τῇ α'
τῶν 'Επιλέκτων.]

(Diogenes Laertius 10.96)

Other instances from this epistle may be seen in Diogenes 10.91,
101(?), 103. To return to the *Epistle to Herodotus*, there is preserved in it
a complex specimen of *Textgeschichte*:

τὸ δὲ ψεῦδος καὶ τὸ διημαρτημένον ἐν τῷ προσδοξαζομένῳ ἀεί
ἐστιν ⟨ἐπὶ τοῦ προσμένοντος⟩ ἐπιμαρτυρηθήσεσθαι ἢ μὴ ἀντι-
μαρτυρηθήσεσθαι, εἶτ' οὐκ ἐπιμαρτυρουμένου ⟨ἢ ἀντιμαρτυ-
ρουμένου⟩ [κατά τινα κίνησιν ἐν ἡμῖν αὐτοῖς συνημμένην τῇ
φανταστικῇ ἐπιβολῇ, διάληψιν δὲ ἔχουσαν, καθ' ἣν τὸ ψεῦδος
γίνεται].

(Diogenes Laertius 10.50)

The additions ⟨ἐπὶ τοῦ προσμένοντος⟩ and ⟨ἢ ἀντιμαρτυρουμένου⟩
were made by Usener; they seem required by the sense. Both omissions are cases of haplography: (1) the copyist's eye skipped from ἐπὶ
to ἐπι-; (2) the homoioteleuton -μαρτυρουμένου caused a visual error.
Of the deleted words [κατά τινα ... γίνεται] Bailey states (in his
edition of Epicurus, p. 197): "After ἐπιμαρτυρουμένου the MSS have
what is clearly a note on τὸ προσδοξαζόμενον derived from the
material of the next section." I give here the section referred to:

τὸ δὲ διημαρτημένον οὐκ ἂν ὑπῆρχεν εἰ μὴ ἐλαμβάνομεν καὶ
ἄλλην τινὰ κίνησιν ἐν ἡμῖν αὐτοῖς συνημμένην μὲν ‹τῇ φανταστικῇ ἐπιβολῇ,› διάληψιν δὲ ἔχουσαν· κατὰ δὲ ταύτην [τὴν συνημμένην τῇ φανταστικῇ ἐπιβολῇ, διάληψιν δὲ ἔχουσαν], ἐὰν μὲν μὴ
ἐπιμαρτυρηθῇ ἢ ἀντιμαρτυρηθῇ, τὸ ψεῦδος γίνεται· ἐὰν δὲ ἐπιμαρτυρηθῇ ἢ μὴ ἀντιμαρτυρηθῇ, τὸ ἀληθές.

(Diogenes Laertius 10.51)

Usener added ‹τῇ φανταστικῇ ἐπιβολῇ› *from the interpolated scholium* in
10.50 cited above. ("The missing dative is supplied with certainty from
the gloss on §50 above. Opinion is closely linked with the ἐπιβολή because it combines images in σύνθεσις, but it differs in that it acts at
random and does not check its conclusions by ἐπιμαρτύρησις and οὐκ
ἀντιμαρτύρησις." Bailey.) In other words, *before* ‹τῇ φανταστικῇ
ἐπιβολῇ› accidentally dropped out, a marginal comment *based on this
sentence* was composed to explain 10.50. It is, therefore, perfectly
reasonable to restore this sentence to its original form on the basis of
the interpolation. (In 10.51 the deleted words [τὴν συνημμένην . . .
ἔχουσαν] are either a scholium [Usener, Bailey] or "tamquam cor-
rectio" [von der Muehll].)

The tenth book of Diogenes Laertius furnishes still another interesting piece of Epicurean *Textgeschichte*:

(a) *Epistle to Menoeceus* (Diogenes Laertius 10.132)

διὸ καὶ φιλοσοφίας τιμιώτερον ὑπάρχει φρόνησις, ἐξ ἧς αἱ λοιπαὶ
πᾶσαι πεφύκασιν ἀρεταί, διδάσκουσα ὡς οὐκ ἔστιν ἡδέως ζῆν
ἄνευ τοῦ φρονίμως καὶ καλῶς καὶ δικαίως, ‹οὐδὲ φρονίμως καὶ
καλῶς καὶ δικαίως› ἄνευ τοῦ ἡδέως.

‹οὐδὲ . . . δικαίως› add. Stephanus

(b) *Κύριαι Δόξαι* 5 (Diogenes Laertius 10.140)

οὐκ ἔστιν ἡδέως ζῆν ἄνευ τοῦ φρονίμως καὶ καλῶς καὶ δικαίως,
‹οὐδὲ φρονίμως καὶ καλῶς καὶ δικαίως› ἄνευ τοῦ ἡδέως.

‹οὐδὲ . . . δικαίως› add. Gassendi

In each passage the same words have accidentally been omitted by
haplography. The sense demanded their restoration, and since the dis-

covery in 1884 of the famous Epicurean inscriptions set up by a certain Diogenes at Oenoanda, the correctness of the solution has been confirmed: [οὐκ ἔστιν ἡδέως ζῆν ἄνευ τοῦ φρονίμ]ως καὶ καλῶς καὶ δικαίως, οὐδὲ φρονίμως καὶ καλῶς καὶ δικα[ίως ἄνευ τοῦ ἡδέως (frag. 54 William=frag. 37 [p. 67] Chilton). It is a bit contrary to probabilities that this same scribal error should have occurred twice in such close proximity, but in textual criticism, if anywhere, Agathon's view is valid: εἰκὸς γὰρ γίνεσθαι πολλὰ καὶ παρὰ τὸ εἰκός. These passages well illustrate the use and limits of parallel passages in establishing the text. The Diogenes inscription has been quite properly adduced to support the insertion ⟨οὐδὲ φρονίμως καὶ καλῶς καὶ δικαίως⟩. It is the final guarantee that Stephanus and Gassendi had recovered not only the sense of the two passages, but in fact the *ipsissima verba*. On the other hand, these two passages, as they have been transmitted in the MSS, are a specimen of *deceptive confirmation*; normally, such agreement would argue for the soundness of both passages. It is only because the MSS furnish an incomplete sense that we can be sure that there is a corruption in both places. Where the sense does not serve as a touchstone, parallels must be used with especial discretion. How deceptive they can be may be seen from a consideration of these verses from the *Phoenissae* of Euripides (1579–1581):

πάντα δ' ἐν ἄματι τῷδε συνάγαγεν,
ὦ πάτερ, ἁμετέροισι δόμοισιν ἄχη θεὸς ὃς
τάδε τελευτᾷ.

(Antigone is addressing Oedipus.) I recently conjectured ἔν' ἄματι τῷδε, "on this *one* day," to contrast with πάντα; the dative of time without a preposition is no difficulty. The following "parallels" may be adduced from Euripides:

(1) ἓν ἦμάρ μ' ὤλβισ', ἓν δ' ἀπώλεσεν

    (*Phoen.* 1689; note that Oedipus is the speaker)

(2) ἀλλ' ἦμαρ ⟨ἕν⟩ τοι μεταβολὰς πολλὰς ἔχει

                                    (frag. 549 Nauck)

(3) τὸν πάντα δ᾽ ὄλβον ἦμαρ ἕν μ᾽ ἀφείλετο

(Hec. 285)

That we are here dealing with a τόπος can be demonstrated from the well-known verses of Sosiphanes, an acknowledged imitator of Euripides:

ὦ δυστυχεῖς μὲν πολλά, παῦρα δ᾽ ὄλβιοι
βροτοί, τί σεμνύνεσθε ταῖς ἐξουσίαις,
ἃς ἕν τ᾽ ἔδωκε φέγγος ἕν τ᾽ ἀφείλετο;

(frag. 3.1–3 Nauck)

On the basis of these passages considered collectively, I would probably still be regarding my ἕν᾽ ἄματι τῷδε a rather likely suggestion, had not Professor Charles Murgia kindly reminded me that the elision of datival -ι is extremely dubious in Attic tragedy. (See Jebb on Sophocles, *OC* 1436, appendix.) Take one more instance, Theognis 91–92:

ὃς δὲ μιῇ γλώσσῃ δίχ᾽ ἔχει νόον, οὗτος ἑταῖρος
δεινός, Κύρν᾽, ἐχθρὸς βέλτερος ἢ φίλος ὤν.

The thought is clear enough, but the simple dative μιῇ γλώσσῃ has no doubt given pause to more readers than myself. It occurred to me that Theognis might have written δ᾽ἐν ἰῇ γλώσσῃ, uncial ΔΕΝΙΗΙ being misread as ΔΕΜΙΗΙ. Compare Semonides frag. 7.27 Diehl, ἢ δύ᾽ ἐν φρεσὶν νοεῖ, and Sallust's *aliud clausum in pectore aliud in lingua promptum habere* (*Cat.* 10.5). The change is facile enough, but a little reflection gives the lie to it. ἴα for μία is not exceptionally rare in Epic and Aeolic verse, but there is not, to my knowledge, a single instance of it in Greek elegiac poetry. For the simple dative compare pseudo-Phocylides, verse 20 γλώσσῃ νοῦν ἐχέμεν, κρυπτὸν λόγον ἐν φρεσὶν ἴσχειν, and verse 48 μὴ δ᾽ ἕτερον κεύθῃς κραδίῃ νόον ἀλλ᾽ ἀγορεύων; Pittacus *ap.* Diogenes Laertius 1.78 πιστὸν γὰρ οὐδὲν γλῶσσα διὰ στόματος / λαλεῖ διχόμυθον ἔχουσα / καρδίᾳ νόημα.

43

§36

It is common knowledge that a great many errors arise from a visual confusion of letters of similar appearance, and I offer a few specimens here. (F. W. Hall, *Companion to Classical Texts*, pp. 158–160, lists the Greek letters which are most commonly confused; his list is useful, but it must be stressed that the probable frequency of a particular confusion is to be learned from the papyri and MSS themselves, not from a handbook list.) Since the substitution of similar letters is the most popular form of conjecture among amateurs, some precautionary remarks are in order. First, errors of sound are more frequent than errors of sight. (This does not necessarily imply that dictation was the normal, or even a widespread, practice. Whenever a person thinks, he pronounces, if only slightly, to himself; scientists can measure such movements of the vocal organs. When one is reading, this "silent" pronunciation is more marked, and it will be recalled that the Greeks and Romans regularly read aloud.) Secondly, the majority of errors due to confusion of letters are superficial and easily detected. Thirdly, and most important, two common practices should be avoided. First, the average person, when confronted with a textual corruption (real or imaginary), will immediately attempt to solve the problem by a process of trial substitution of similar letters. This game of checkers will seldom lead anywhere in the case of a serious corruption and is certainly not to be regarded as "critical method." The sense demanded by the passage and the style of the author or literary genre are the touchstones of a true conjecture, not similar-looking letters. Secondly, when a corruption can be legitimately explained by the *ductus litterarum*, there is a neatness and economy to the solution which makes it especially convincing and appealing. This is as it should be, but it ought not to seduce us into committing a frequent fallacy—I mean the unconscious tendency to refuse to accept a conjecture, howsoever convincing on grounds of sense and style, if a precise *paleographical* explanation of the corruption is not forthcoming. By no means is every error due to the misreading

44

of letters. The melancholy fact is that there are numerous passages where scholars have correctly emended the text, but where the corruption remains unexplained. In not a few instances, such emendations have later been fully confirmed by new papyrus discoveries.

The following examples illustrate some *uncial* confusions, which so often are important for the demonstration of an archetype (i.e., if all the minuscule MSS of a work contain common errors which are due to the misreading of uncial script, it normally follows that all the extant MSS ultimately derive from one minuscule exemplar copied from an uncial MS or MSS). The principles involved, *mutatis mutandis*, apply to minuscule errors as well.

§37. Anacreon frag. 57c Page (= 32D)

ἐμὲ γὰρ †λόγων εἵνεκα παῖδες ἂν φιλέοιεν·
χαρίεντα μὲν γὰρ ἄιδω, χαρίεντα δ' οἶδα λέξαι.

ἄιδω Valckenaer : διδῶ codd.

διδῶ is meaningless and unmetrical; the error arose from the misreading of an uncial alpha as delta: ΑΙΔΩ : ΔΙΔΩ.

§38. Euripides *Cyclops* 676–677

ὁ ξένος, ἵν' ὀρθῶς ἐκμάθῃς, μ' ἀπώλεσεν,
ὁ μιαρός, ὅς μοι δοὺς τὸ πῶμα κατέκλυσεν.

κατέκλυσε Canter : κατέκαυσε L P : κατέσπασε p

Here clearly ΚΛΥΣΕ was misread as ΚΑΥΣΕ; the copyist was psychologically conditioned for the slip by earlier occurrences of καίω in this play (ἐκκάειν v. 633, ἐκκαίετε v. 657, καιέτω v. 659). κατέσπασε, the guess of a later hand in P, was probably inspired by the wrestling image of the following verse (δεινὸς γὰρ οἶνος καὶ παλαίεσθαι βαρύς).

§39. *Carmina Popularia* 7.5-6 Page (= 43D)

ἀμέρα καὶ ἤδη· τὸ φῶς
διὰ τᾶς θυρίδος οὐκ εἰσορῆις;

εἰσορῆις Meineke : ἐκόρης

Confusion of εἰς and ἐκ is uncial (ΕΙϹ : ΕΚ); the iota adscript, of course, was often omitted in medieval MSS. (In uncial MSS iota adscript had ceased to be written from about 100 B.C.)

§40. Arrian *Anabasis* 1.19.9

. . . ἐκεῖθεν δὲ ἐπισιτισάμενοι αὖθις ἐπέπλεον τῇ Μιλήτῳ· καὶ τὰς μὲν πολλὰς τῶν νεῶν πρὸ τοῦ λιμένος ἐν μετεώρῳ παρέταξαν, εἴ πῃ ἐκκαλέσαιντο ἐς τὸ πέλαγος τοὺς Μακεδόνας, πέντε δὲ αὐτῶν εἰσέπλευσαν ἐς τὸν μεταξὺ τῆς τε †ἄλλης† νήσου καὶ τοῦ στρατοπέδου λιμένα . . .

The reference to the "other island" is unintelligible in context. Palmerius long ago saw that the island meant was Lade, once the site of a famous battle in the Ionian revolt. ΛΑΔ and ΑΛΛ are easily confused, and psychological factors come into play. The scribe's mind unconsciously seizes upon that which is more familiar (ἄλλης being of far more frequent occurrence than λάδης).

§41. Martial *Liber Spectaculorum* 21.7-8

ipse sed ingrato iacuit laceratus ab urso
†haec tamen res est facta ita pictoria†

During a representation on the stage of the Orpheus legend, an accident occurred. The actor playing Orpheus was killed by a bear! Housman (*CR* 15 [1901] 154–155) set the last line right:

haec tantum res est facta παρ' ἱστορίαν.

"This alone happened contrary to the story." As Housman pointed out, *tantum* and *tamen* were both abbreviated t̄m; the crucial corruption resulted from a misreading of Greek uncials as Latin script: ΠΑΡΙϹΤΟΡΙᾹ→ITAPICTORIA. (Buecheler anticipated Housman—as Housman himself scrupulously records—in perceiving that ICTORIA was in fact the Greek ἱστορία, but he did not succeed in recovering the correct verse.) It should be noted that this is by no means an isolated instance of the misreading of Greek letters as Latin in Latin MSS.

§42. Hippocrates *De Victu* 2.47 *ad fin.*

νήσσης δὲ καὶ τῶν ἄλλων ὁκόσα ἐν ἕλεσι διαιτῆται ἢ ἐν ὕδασι, πάντα ὑγρά.

W. H. S. Jones in his Loeb edition of Hippocrates (vol. 4 p. 321) records that "θ [= Codex Vindobonensis med. IV] has εαεσι—an interesting survival of a mistake made when the manuscripts were in uncials; ΕΛΕϹΙ and ΕΑΕϹΙ."

§43. Diogenes Laertius 10.27

καὶ διὰ τοῦτο καὶ πολλάκις ταὐτὰ γέγραφε καὶ τὸ ἐπελθόν, καὶ ἀδιόρθωτα †εἷλκε† τῷ ἐπείγεσθαι.

Cobet saw that ΕΙΛΚΕ was an uncial slip for ΕΙΑΚΕ (i.e. εἴακε).

§44. Plutarch *Moralia* 361F (*De Iside et Osiride* 28)

Πτολεμαῖος δ' ὁ Σωτὴρ ὄν⟨αρ⟩ εἶδε τὸν ἐν Σινώπῃ τοῦ Πλού- τωνος κολοσσόν, οὐκ ἐπιστάμενος οὐδ' ἑωρακὼς πρότερον οἷος τὴν μορφὴν ⟨ἦν⟩, κελεύοντα κομίσαι τὴν ταχίστην αὐτὸν εἰς

Ἀλεξάνδρειαν. ἀγνοοῦντι δ' αὐτῷ καὶ ἀποροῦντι, ποῦ καθίδρυ-
ται, καὶ διηγουμένῳ τοῖς φίλοις τὴν ὄψιν, εὑρέθη πολυπλανὴς
ἄνθρωπος ὄνομα Σωσίβιος, ἐν Σινώπῃ φάμενος ἑωρακέναι
τοιοῦτον κολοσσόν, οἷον ὁ βασιλεὺς ἰδεῖν ἔδοξεν.

ὄν⟨αρ⟩ εἶδε is the ingenious correction of William Baxter (1650–1723)
for ἀνεῖλε of the MSS, which makes no sense, whereas it is clear from
the passage that Ptolemy has seen a vision. Note τὴν ὄψιν and ἰδεῖν
ἔδοξεν (δοκεῖν is the verb regularly used for dreams and visions; compare LSJ s.v. δοκέω I.1). This detail of the story is confirmed by Tacitus, *Historiae* 4.83.1 ... *per quietem* ... The corruption began from a
misreading of ΕΙΔΕ as ΕΙΛΕ.

§45. Plutarch *Moralia* 372B (*De Iside et Osiride* 52)

... καὶ τῇ τριακάδι τοῦ Ἐπιφὶ μηνὸς ἑορτάζουσιν ὀφθαλμῶν
Ὥρου γενέθλιον ...

γενέθλιον Bentley : γενέσθαι ὂν

In uncial script (and only in uncial script) the corruption is self-evident:
ΓΕΝΕΘΛΙΟΝ→ΓΕΝΕϹΘΑΙΟΝ.

§46. Plutarch *Moralia* 388C (*De E apud Delphos* 8)

ὡς οὖν ἄρρενός τε τοῦ πρώτου καὶ θήλεος ὁμιλίᾳ τὰ πέντε γιγ-
νόμενα γάμον οἱ Πυθαγόρειοι προσεῖπον.

ὁμιλίᾳ Wyttenbach : ὃ μὴ διὰ Γ : ὁμοιότητι O

"The Pythagoreans thus named the number five 'Marriage' as having
been produced by the union of the first male and first female number."

48

The Γ family has faithfully preserved the (corrupt) archetypal reading; ὁμοιότητι is, as we shall see, a conscious conjecture. The uncial exemplar had OMIΛIA which was misread and falsely divided as ὃ μὴ διὰ (μὴ of course is a simple itacism which may already have occurred in the uncial MS). *Moralia* 388A above both confirms ὁμιλία (which is to be understood in a sexual sense) and reveals why someone wrote by conjecture ὁμοιότητι for the corrupt ὃ μὴ διὰ:

> ἀρχὴν δὲ τοῦ μὲν ἀρτίου τὰ δύο τοῦ δὲ περιττοῦ τὰ τρία ποιοῦν-
> ται, τὰ δὲ πέντε γεννᾶται τούτων πρὸς ἀλλήλους μειγνυμένων
> . . . καὶ γάμος ἐπωνόμασται τῇ τοῦ ἀρτίου πρὸς τὸ θῆλυ περιτ-
> τοῦ δ' αὖ πρὸς τὸ ἄρρεν ὁμοιότητι.

Five was called γάμος because (1) it was the product of the union (ὁμιλία) of two and three (τούτων πρὸς ἀλλήλους μειγνυμένων) and (2) because the even number (two) and the odd number (three) bore a resemblance (ὁμοιότης) respectively to female and male, but *not* because of a resemblance between ὁ πρῶτος ἄρρην ἀριθμός (= 3) and ὁ πρῶτος θῆλυς ἀριθμός (= 2) to *each other*. In 388C therefore ὁμοιότητι does not give the required sense and stands exposed as a conscious conjecture. (Note that the Γ family, by faithfully transmitting ὃ μὴ διὰ, meaningless though it was, made it much easier for modern scholars to recover what Plutarch wrote than it would have been if all the MSS had the "improvement" ὁμοιότητι. This is very frequently to be taken into account in evaluating MSS.)

Plutarch *Moralia* 52B is a very illustrative example of a conscious conjecture that has succeeded in deceiving more than one modern editor:

> ὁ μὲν γὰρ πίθηκος, ὡς ἔοικε, μιμεῖσθαι τὸν ἄνθρωπον ἐπιχειρῶν
> ἁλίσκεται συγκινούμενος καὶ συνορχούμενος . . .

So print, for example, Bernardakis and Babbitt, neither of whom records a variant. But there is one: a few MSS preserve the marginal variant ὦτος (= "horned owl") for πίθηκος. ὦτος is the correct reading and Paton rightly prints it in his Teubner edition. Someone, not under-standing the reference to the ὦτος here, deliberately changed the word to πίθηκος, the "mimetic" animal *par excellence*. ὦτος is confirmed by another passage in the *Moralia*, 961E:

> ὁ δ᾽ ὦτος αὖ πάλιν ἁλίσκεται γοητευόμενος, ὀρχουμένων ἐν ὄψει
> μεθ᾽ ἡδονῆς ἅμα ῥυθμῷ γλιχόμενος τοὺς ὤμους συνδιαφέρειν.

Helmbold's note on this passage reads as follows: "*Cf. Mor.* 52 B (where the L.C.L., probably wrongly, reads 'the ape'); 705 A; Athenaeus, 390 f; Aelian, *De Natura Animal.* xv. 28; Pliny, *Nat. Hist.* x. 68; Aristotle, *Historia Animal.* viii. 13 (597 B 22 ff.) and the other references of Hubert at *Mor.* 705 A and Gulick on Athenaeus, 629 f . . ." The evidence in support of ὦτος at *Mor.* 52B seems to me quite decisive; Plutarch there wrote ὦτος. (Whether the marginal variant ὦτος in a few MSS at 52B represents a genuine MS tradition is another question. I should guess that the archetype had only πίθηκος, a false conjecture, which had ejected ὦτος, and that later in the medieval tradition ὦτος was reintroduced by a learned conjecture which happened to be correct.)

§47. Euripides *Phoenissae* 263-264

> ὃ καὶ δέδοικα μή με δικτύων ἔσω
> λαβόντες οὐκ ἐκφρῶσ᾽ ἀναίμακτον χρόα.

οὐκ ἐκφρῶσ᾽ Bergk : οὐ μεθῶσ᾽ M : οὐ μεθῶσιν rell.

Bergk recovered the reading οὐκ ἐκφρῶσ᾽ from a scholium to this passage: ἡ μὲν γραφὴ οὐκ ἐκφρῶσιν. οἱ οὖν ὑποκριταὶ διὰ τὸ δυσέκφορον μεταπλάττουσι τὴν λέξιν. καὶ Φιλόξενος ἐν τῷ περὶ μονοσυλλάβων ῥημάτων, ὅτε διαλαμβάνει περὶ τοῦ φρῶ, ταύτην τὴν χρῆσίν φησιν. (Apparently, as Paley observes, the actors found it difficult to distinguish in pronunciation ἐκφρῶσ᾽ and ἐκφέρωσ᾽; see further Merry on Aristophanes *Vespae* 162, where Buttmann's ἔκφρες is now generally read for ἔκφερε of the MSS.) This scholium has the ring of authentic learned tradition; οὐ μεθῶσ᾽ is in itself unexceptionable and would not inspire a grammarian to invent the comments preserved by the scholiast. We must conclude that οὐ μεθῶσ' is exactly what the scholiast states it is—a deliberate change. The correctness of Bergk's suggestion seems to receive further confirmation from an entry in Photius' *Lexicon*: οὐκ ἐκφρῶσιν· οὐκ ἐξαφῶσι. Σοφοκλῆς. There is general agreement among scholars that in this entry Σοφοκλῆς is probably a slip for Εὐριπίδης and that the reference is to the *Phoenissae* passage. In support of this, I might call attention to the fact that neither φρέω nor any one of its compounds (δια-, εἰσ-, ἐκ-, ἐπεισ-) ever occurs in Aeschylus or Sophocles; these verbs are found rather in prose writers (thirteen examples cited in LSJ), the comic writers (six examples in LSJ), and Euripides, who uses εἰσφρέω once and ἐπεισφρέω four times (see LSJ). (Hesychius gives three further instances of indeterminate provenience, and the *Suda* one.) Compare my comments above, sec. 31, on Sophocles *Trachiniae* 82–85.

False ascriptions of citations such as this one from Photius' *Lexicon* are nothing unusual in the Greek grammatical tradition; they are rather to be expected. For example, the scholium to *Iliad* 15.207 (ἐσθλὸν καὶ τὸ τέτυκται, ὅτ' ἄγγελος αἴσιμα εἰδῇ) begins καὶ Εὐριπίδης "ἐν ἀγγέλῳ γὰρ κυπτὸς ὀρθοῦται λόγος." The quotation is in fact not from Euripides at all; it is verse 773 of Aeschylus' *Choephori*. (Eustathius [p. 1013.12], who does not appear to be independent here, repeats the error.) Yet this Homeric scholium, despite its garbled reference, is invaluable to us, for it alone has preserved correctly Aeschylus' verse, which is corrupt in the direct MS tradition (represented by M=codex Mediceus Laurentianus 32.9). M transmits not ὀρθοῦται λόγος, which is clearly right, but ὀρθούσηι φρενί, a mechanical blunder caused by ἀγαθούσηι φρενί of the preceding verse. Furthermore, κυπτὸς of the Homer codex, Venetus B, may well be correct; most of the MSS containing Homeric scholia, Eustathius, and the direct MS tradition of Aeschylus all have κρυπτός, but the meaning of κρυπτὸς ὀρθοῦται λόγος has long been a puzzle. κυπτὸς ὀρθοῦται λόγος, "a crooked report is made straight," is a readily intelligible expression and is printed by many editors of Aeschylus. LSJ do not recognize the existence of κυπτός, -ή, -όν, except in the entry from Hesychius κυπτόν· ταπεινούμενον. (Here, incidentally, they are almost certainly in error; the *participial* definition ταπεινούμενον makes it likely that Alberti was correct in seeing here a biblical gloss to LXX, Baruch 2.18, ὃ βαδίζει κύπτον καὶ ἀσθενοῦν, and emending to κύπτον, the participle of κύπτω.) Nevertheless κυπτός would be a perfectly regular formation; compare βάπτω/βαπτός, καλύπτω/καλυπτός, κρύπτω/κρυπτός. The case for κυπτός in Aeschylus is set forth clearly and in detail by M. MacLaren in *CP* 27 (1932) 357–358. This is an especially illustrative instance of false ascription, for we cannot argue that this verse was proverbial and used by both Aeschylus and Euripides, and that hence the scholiast's statement strictly is not false. (Advocates of such a line of reasoning have never been far to seek.) If κρυπτός is the correct lection, the verse is too obscure to be proverbial; if κυπτός is correct, the *recherché* diction seems to stamp the verse as the creation of a single poet. It is essential to distinguish between words that have a *proverbial ring* to them (as here) and actual *proverbs* (which may turn up in several authors). Thus there was a Greek proverb "be mad with the mad," i.e. "when in Rome, do as the Romans do"; Galen (2.56–57 Kühn) explicitly attests its existence: ... ἀλλ', ὡς ἡ παροιμία φησί, μαινομένοις ἀναγκασθέντες συμμανῆναι. When Theognis, verse 313, writes ἐν μὲν μαινομένοις μάλα μαίνομαι, he is consciously echoing the proverb (as I have demonstrated in *CR* 13 [1963] 131–132). In one form or another, this proverb has been preserved in an Attic scolion, the comic poet Callias, Menander, and the *Suda*. It no doubt was taken over into literature from common speech. At other times, a proverb is repeated from an earlier author with a definite literary allusion. *Odyssey* 17.218 was undoubtedly a familiar verse— ὡς αἰεὶ τὸν ὁμοῖον ἄγει θεὸς ὡς τὸν ὁμοῖον; Callimachus (frag. 178.7–10 Pfeiffer) explicitly refers to it:

ἦν δὲ γενέθλην
"Ικιος, ᾧ ξυνὴν εἶχον ἐγὼ κλισίην
οὐκ ἐπιτάξ, ἀλλ' αἶνος Ὁμηρικός, αἰὲν ὁμοῖον
ὡς θεός, οὐ ψευδής, ἐς τὸν ὁμοῖον ἄγει.

(It is interesting to note in passing that Callimachus writes ἐς τὸν ὁμοῖον; some of the Homeric MSS—supported by Plato, [Aristotle],

"Hippocrates"—give ὡς τὸν ὁμοῖον, which, if genuine, is the only instance of ὡς used as a preposition in Homer. The usage is mostly an Attic one.) Again, in his *Hymn to Zeus*, verse 8, Callimachus incorporates part of a saying traditionally attributed to Epimenides (frag. 1 Diels–Kranz), the well-known "Κρῆτες ἀεὶ ψεῦσται." The complete verse has been preserved in the Pauline Epistle to Titus 1.12: εἶπέν τις ἐξ αὐτῶν [sc. τῶν Κρητῶν] ἴδιος αὐτῶν προφήτης· Κρῆτες ἀεὶ ψεῦσται, κακὰ θηρία, γαστέρες ἀργαί (for the traditional epic phrasing compare *Iliad* 24.260–261 and Hesiod *Theogony* 26). This verse is also alluded to in a cenotaph epigram ascribed to Cn. Cornelius Lentulus Gaetulicus, *Anthologia Palatina* 7.275.5–6:

> τὸν ψεύσταν δέ με τύμβον ἐπὶ χθονὶ θέντο. τί θαῦμα,
> Κρῆτες ὅπου ψεῦσται καὶ Διὸς ἔστι τάφος;

Such literary allusions are not at all uncommon; Pindar, for instance, alludes to Hesiod in *Isthmian* 6.66–68:

> Λάμπων δὲ μελέταν
> ἔργοις ὀπάζων Ἡσιό-
> δου μάλα τιμᾷ τοῦτ᾽ ἔπος,
> υἱοῖσί τε φράζων παραινεῖ . . .

Compare *Works and Days* 412: μελέτη δέ τοι ἔργον ὀφέλλει. Bacchylides (5.191–194 Snell) cites a saying of Hesiod (frag. 202 Rzach) not otherwise known; see Snell's edition of Bacchylides, *praefatio* p. 22, for literary imitations and allusions in that poet. When a literary proverb has been used by more than one writer, the source of the citation may become obscured. We may call upon St. Paul for an illustration of this. In 1 Corinthians 15.33 he writes φθείρουσιν ἤθη χρηστὰ ὁμιλίαι κακαί. There is no doubt that this is a quotation; the words are in fact an iambic trimeter verse which was very famous in antiquity (in Paul χρήσθ᾽ has been "trivialized" to the unmetrical χρηστὰ). ["It was not uncommon (cf. inscriptions) to neglect making elisions in writing verse, as in writing prose. Perhaps it had something to do with facilitating the reading of the *scriptio continua*." B.E.] But whom is Paul quoting? He himself may not have known, for the verse was probably

53

already in his day a commonplace; compare Diodorus Siculus 16.54: ταῖς πονηραῖς ὁμιλίαις διέφθειρε τὰ ἤθη τῶν ἀνθρώπων. The ancient sources are in discrepancy here; some attributed the line to Euripides and some to Menander. For a complete list of *testimonia* see Euripides frag. 1024 Nauck, and Menander frag. 187 Koerte. According to Koerte, "Versum Euripidi deberi, a Menandro in Thaidem translatum esse paene certum est." Another proverb found in Menander (frag. 59.4 Koerte), though certainly not original with him, is ἀνερρίφθω κύβος. Aristophanes (frag. 673 Kock) shows a variation of it: φράζε τοίνυν, ὡς ἐγώ σοι πᾶς ἀνέρριμμαι κύβος. There is no doubt that ἀνερρίφθω κύβος was, as Koerte calls it, a "proverbium notissimum." Appian (*BC* 2.35) and Plutarch (*Pompey* 60, *Caesar* 32) both state that Caesar exclaimed ἀνερρίφθω κύβος at his famous crossing of the Rubicon. Plutarch is quite explicit. In his *Life of Caesar* he states: τοῦτο δὴ τὸ κοινὸν τοῖς εἰς τύχας ἐμβαίνουσιν ἀπόρους καὶ τόλμας προοίμιον ὑπειπών, "'Ανερρίφθω κύβος," ὥρμησε πρὸς τὴν διάβασιν; and in his *Life of Pompey* he states: καὶ τοσοῦτον μόνον Ἑλληνιστὶ πρὸς τοὺς παρόντας ἐκβοήσας, "'Ανερρίφθω κύβος," διεβίβαζε τὸν στρατόν. The following facts thus appear: (1) ἀνερρίφθω κύβος was a common saying uttered *before* (προοίμιον) undertaking a risky and doubtful venture; (2) Caesar's terse comment at the Rubicon was made (a) in Greek (b) *before* he crossed the stream. He was in fact quoting a Greek proverb of common currency. Suetonius, in his *Divus Iulius* 32, gives us the story in Latin dress; the MSS read

> tunc Caesar: "eatur," inquit, "quo deorum ostenta et inimicorum iniquitas vocat. iacta alea est."

Strictly speaking the "die was not cast" until *after* Caesar crossed the Rubicon; *iacta alea est* is slightly illogical. But this distinction must not and need not be pressed. It is clear from the evidence presented above that Suetonius, who certainly knew the famous story, is here translating the Greek proverb ἀνερρίφθω κύβος; the Greek has a perfect *imperative* and Suetonius rendered it by a Latin perfect imperative: *iacta alea esto. est* of the MSS is nothing but a trivialization of the commonest sort. The rare perfect imperative corrupted to a familiar perfect indicative. Centuries ago the great Erasmus conjectured *iacta alea esto*; the general reluctance of editors of Suetonius to this day to print *esto* is incomprehensible to me. Lest there be any who, *pace* Plutarch, do not think that the *perfect* ἀνερρίφθω κύβος can be said of an act not yet begun, I give here a larger extract from the Menander fragment cited above:

A.   οὐ γαμεῖς, ἂν νοῦν ἔχῃς,
τοῦτον καταλείπων τὸν βίον· γεγάμηκα γὰρ
αὐτός· διὰ τοῦτό σοι παραινῶ μὴ γαμεῖν.
B.   δεδογμένον τὸ πρᾶγμ'· ἀνερρίφθω κύβος.
A.   πέραινε, σωθείης δὲ κτλ.

§48. *Iliad* 13.656–659

τὸν μὲν Παφλαγόνες μεγαλήτορες ἀμφεπένοντο,
ἐς δίφρον δ' ἀνέσαντες ἄγον προτὶ Ἴλιον ἱρὴν
ἀχνύμενοι· μετὰ δέ σφι πατὴρ κίε δάκρυα λείβων,
ποινὴ δ' οὔ τις παιδὸς ἐγίγνετο τεθνηῶτος.

These verses refer to the mortally wounded Harpalio, son of Pylaemenes. Since Pylaemenes had been killed in *Iliad* 5.576–579, the poet has involved himself in an inconsistency, which was already noticed in antiquity. Aristophanes obelized verses 658–659 as spurious, and Aristarchus concluded that either these verses were not genuine or that the Pylaemenes mentioned at 5.576 was a different person—despite the fact that in 5.577 Pylaemenes is called ἀρχὸν Παφλαγόνων and in 13.643 he is referred to as βασιλῆος (viz. of the Paphlagonians). A scholium in A (= codex Venetus 454) preserves an ancient variant reading for μετὰ δέ σφι (verse 658): ἔνιοι δὲ πιθανῶς μεταγράφουσι "μετὰ δ' οὔ σφι." There can be no doubt that this lection, its antiquity notwithstanding, is nothing but a deliberate attempt to remove the contradiction. An even more patent example of tampering with the

Homeric text may be seen at *Iliad* 9.450–454, where Phoenix is speaking:

> τὴν αὐτὸς φιλέεσκεν, ἀτιμάζεσκε δ' ἄκοιτιν,
> μητέρ' ἐμήν· ἡ δ' αἰὲν ἐμὲ λισσέσκετο γούνων
> παλλακίδι προμιγῆναι, ἵν' ἐχθήρειε γέροντα.
> τῇ πιθόμην καὶ ἔρεξα· πατὴρ δ' ἐμὸς αὐτίκ' ὀϊσθεὶς
> πολλὰ κατηρᾶτο, στυγερὰς δ' ἐπεκέκλετ' Ἐρινῦς . . .

A scholium in codex A records that Aristodemus of Nysa—offended by the moral tone of the passage—"contrived" (ἐπενόησε) for verse 453 the reading τῇ οὐ πιθόμην οὐδ' ἔρεξα (i.e. ἔρξα). The scholium continues πρὸ δὲ αὐτοῦ Σωσιφάνης [frag. 6 Nauck] τὴν τοιαύτην εὗρε γραφήν· καὶ Εὐριπίδης δὲ ἀναμάρτητον εἰσάγει τὸν ἥρωα ἐν τῷ Φοίνικι. Eustathius, p. 763.9–12, records the same information. [It seems to have gone unnoticed that Heyne questioned the soundness of Σωσιφάνης here. The note to this passage of Homer in his *Homeri Carmina*, vol. 5 p. 626, reads in part: ". . . Excogitaverat iam ante eum [sc. Aristodemum] *Sosiphanes* (tragicum hoc nomine fuisse constat; sed leg. *Sosigenes* idem grammaticus cuius ἔκδοσις Homeri fuit) eandem scripturam."]

The reading τῇ οὐ πιθόμην οὐδ' ἔρξα is, of course, immediately exposed by the context as a conscious rewriting. As to Aristodemus' merits as a critic, I would merely remind the reader that this man may claim as one of his more remarkable achievements the uncommon feat of successfully convincing himself that Homer was a Roman. (For his reasons see the sixth *vita Homeri* in T. W. Allen's OCT *Homeri Opera*, vol. 5 p. 251.18–23.)

§49

There is an interesting example of conscious alteration of the text in the Old Testament. In the first book of Samuel (= 1 Kings in the *Septuaginta*), the thirteenth chapter begins, according to the Hebrew MSS, as follows: "Saul was a child of one year when he began to reign, and he reigned two years over Israel." This is of course nonsense; the Authorized (= King James) Version renders "Saul reigned one year; and when he had reigned two years over Israel . . ."; this makes sense, but biblical scholars have long since been in agreement that this meaning cannot be gotten out of the Hebrew. The fact is that the Hebrew MSS (which, out of reverence, were faithfully and carefully recopied for centuries, obvious errors and all) are corrupt here, and the critics are now inclined to believe that something has dropped out of the text. In the Revised Standard Version, for example, the verse is printed "Saul was . . . years old when he began to reign; and he reigned . . . and two years over Israel." See further S. Goldman, *Samuel, Hebrew Text and English Translation with an Introduction and Commentary* (London and Bournemouth 1951) *ad loc.* To come to the Greek Old Testament (i.e. the *Septuaginta*), we find that this verse has been omitted. We must assume that the omission was deliberate; the verse in the Hebrew was seen to be meaningless and the difficulty was circumvented by simply not translating it. The history of this verse does not stop here, though. In two later revisions of the *Septuaginta*, those of Origen and of Lucian of Antioch, the verse is found: υἱὸς ἐνιαυτοῦ Σαουλ ἐν τῷ βασιλεύειν αὐτὸν καὶ δύο ἔτη ἐβασίλευσεν ἐπὶ Ισραηλ. However, for υἱὸς ἐνιαυτοῦ these two versions also show the variant reading υἱὸς τριάκοντα ἐτῶν, which must be a deliberate conjecture. The guess is in itself improbable, since, when Saul began to reign, his son Jonathan was already old enough to be a commander in battle (see verse 3). The reason for the conjecture "thirty" is perhaps to be sought in the Greek system of numerical notation. The symbol for one is Α, for thirty Λ. The stages in the history of this verse may be summarized as follows:

1. The corrupt Hebrew original, in which it is stated that Saul was a year old when he began to reign.
2. The standard *Septuaginta* translation into Greek, which omitted the verse.
3. Two revisions (Origen and Lucian) of the *Septuaginta*, which restored the verse from the Hebrew.
4. Conscious "correction" of the Greek revisions, whereby the numeral 30 replaced the numeral 1.

Since confusion of uncial alpha (= 1) and lambda (= 30) is so common, it is instructive to speculate on how many modern editors would have printed υἱὸς τριάκοντα ἐτῶν, if there had survived only the Greek MSS with the two variants, and not the original Hebrew ones, which prove that corruption is present here and that υἱὸς ἐνιαυτοῦ must be the pristine form of the Greek (revised) translation.

The Greeks themselves were fully aware that their system of numerical notation readily lent itself to corruption; to demonstrate this I print here a seldom read passage from the *De Antidotis* of Galen (14.31–32 Kühn):

> . . . τὰ δὲ δὴ βιβλία τὰ κατὰ τὰς βιβλιοθήκας ἀποκείμενα, τὰ τῶν ἀριθμῶν ἔχοντα σημεῖα, ῥᾳδίως διαστρέφεται . . . διὰ τοῦτο ἐγώ, καθάπερ ὁ Μενεκράτης ἔγραψε βιβλίον ἐπιγράψας Ὁλογράμματα αὐτοκράτορος, καθότι τὰ μὲν ἑπτὰ διὰ δυοῖν γέγραπται συλλαβῶν, οὐ διὰ τοῦ ζ´ μόνον, τὰ δὲ εἴκοσι διὰ τριῶν, οὐ διὰ τοῦ κ´ μόνον, τὰ δὲ τριάκοντα διὰ τεττάρων, οὐ διὰ τοῦ λ´ μόνον, καὶ τἄλλα ὁμοίως, οὕτω ποιήσω καὶ αὐτός. ἐπαινῶ δὲ καὶ τὸν Ἀνδρόμαχον ἐμμέτρως γράψαντα τὴν Θηριακὴν αὐτήν, ὥσπερ καὶ ἄλλοι τινές. ὁ δὲ Δαμοκράτης καὶ τἄλλα πάντα διὰ μέτρων ἔγραψεν ὀρθῶς ποιήσας. ἥκιστα γὰρ οἱ πανοῦργοι δύνανται διαστρέφειν αὐτά.

(The similar passage in Galen 13.995–996 Kühn should be compared.)

Thus, in the Samuel text, my suggestion is that the conjecture τριάκοντα ἐτῶν *may* have been made by someone influenced at least in part by an awareness that the symbols for "one" and "thirty" were often confused. It is unnecessary to assume—nor do I suggest it for a moment —that the *corrector* actually found the reading ΥΙΟC Ᾱ ΕΝΙΑΥΤΟῩ in any MS. Indeed, the fact should not be overlooked that there is another possible explanation of the number thirty here; it may be due to nothing but a frivolous attempt at parallelism with the statement made about David in LXX, 2 Regg. 5.4: υἱὸς τριάκοντα ἐτῶν Δαυιδ ἐν τῷ βασιλεῦσαι [βασιλεύειν Origen, Lucian!] αὐτὸν καὶ τεσσαράκοντα ἔτη ἐβασίλευσεν. What is certain is that τριάκοντα, whatever motivated the editor to write this particular numeral, must be a conscious

58

—and erroneous—change. Finally, I would point out that the substitution of a different word for "year" (ἐνιαυτοῦ/ἐτῶν) is a further indication of deliberate tampering. Contrast for example, LXX, 3 *Regg.* 14.21: υἱὸς τεσσαράκοντα καὶ ἑνὸς ἐνιαυτῶν Ροβοαμ ἐν τῷ βασιλεύειν αὐτὸν . . . The plural ἔτη is far more frequent than ἐνιαυτοί in Greek prose. The reason for this is that in origin the two words were not synonyms, as may be seen from such phrases as ἔτος ἦλθε περιπλομένων ἐνιαυτῶν (*Od.* 1.16) and χρονίους ἐτῶν παλαιῶν ἐνιαυτούς (Ar. *Ranae* 347). According to LSJ s.v., ἐνιαυτός originally meant "anniversary," "cycle," "period"; its use as a synonym for ἔτος seems to be a later, secondary meaning. Hermann Diels, *Neue Jahrb.* 33 (1914) 2 n. 1, believed that the original meaning of the word was "summer solstice"; in this he was following the conclusions of C. Brugmann, *Indo-Germ. Forsch.* 15 (1903) 87–93.

§50. Heraclides *Epitoma De Atheniensium Republica* 8 (11)

εἰσὶ δὲ καὶ ἐννέα ἄρχοντες. θεσμοθέται ἕξ, οἳ δοκιμασθέντες ὀμνύουσι δικαίως ἄρξειν καὶ δῶρα μὴ λήψεσθαι κτλ.

ἕξ, οἳ Coraes : καὶ οἱ vel sim. libri

(This *Epitome* is conveniently printed in various editions of Aristotle's *Constitution of Athens,* e.g. Kenyon's and Sandys'.) Coraes' emendation is certain; the reference is to the *six* junior archons at Athens, whose official title was θεσμοθέται. The error was caused by a misreading of the abbreviation for ἕξ, namely ϛ (the so-called "stigma" form of digamma); καί, the most frequently abbreviated word in Greek MSS, has as its commonest form of abbreviation a sign which is easily confused with stigma.

§51. Euripides *Electra* 476–477

ἄορι δ᾽ ἐν φονίῳ τετραβάμονες ἵπποι ἔπαλ-
λον, κελαινὰ δ᾽ ἀμφὶ νῶθ᾽ ἵετο κόνις.

ἄορι δ᾽ ἐν Musgrave Hartung : ἐν δὲ δορὶ

These verses are from a choral description of Achilles' armor; ἐν δὲ δορὶ (δόρει Hermann) of the MSS would involve a mention of artistic representations on *spears* which is unexampled. The depiction of such a scene as this on a spear (shaft or head) is in itself physically improbable. The correction ἄορι δ᾽ ἐν makes excellent sense and, appearances to the contrary, is in reality a simple and slight change. The corruption involved two steps: (1) ΑΟΡΙ was misread as ΔΟΡΙ, a far more familiar word; (2) the resultant δορὶ δ᾽ ἐν was unconsciously transposed to the more normal word order ἐν δὲ δορὶ (this change may have been influenced by verse 464 above which begins ἐν δὲ μέσῳ κατέλαμπε σάκει). Of course, the two stages of the corruption may just as easily have taken place in the reverse order. (See further Denniston's discussion in his edition of the play.)

ἄορ is not found elsewhere in the extant remains of Greek tragedy. It ought to be recognized that this certainty lends no positive support to the probability of this conjecture, for Attic Greek tragedy perfected a peculiar—one might almost say technical—diction of its own. The objection (which scholars do not seem to have noticed) is not decisive. ἄορ is a Homeric word and Homeric language pervades all Greek poetry, tragedy included.

A second example of this identical corruption of ᾽ΑΟΡΙ to ΔΟΡΊ may be seen in Nonnus *Dionysiaca* 18.288:

> . . . φονίῳ σέο θύρσῳ
> τόσσον ἀριστεύεις, ὅσσον δορὶ μάρναται ῎Αρης.

Here Koechly corrected ὅσσον δορί to ὅσον ἄορι, a correction which seems confirmed by Nonnus' strict metrical practice. See Paul Maas, *Greek Metre*, sec. 93 (where, however, Maas wrongly reports the MS reading to be ὅσον δορί).

§52. Plato *Hippias Maior* 289A

Ὦ ἄνθρωπε, ἀγνοεῖς ὅτι τὸ τοῦ Ἡρακλείτου εὖ ἔχει, ὡς ἄρα
"Πιθήκων ὁ κάλλιστος αἰσχρὸς ἀνθρώπων γένει συμβάλλειν,"
[= frag. 82 Diels–Kranz] καὶ χυτρῶν ἡ καλλίστη αἰσχρὰ
παρθένων γένει συμβάλλειν, ὥς φησιν Ἱππίας ὁ σοφός.

ἀνθρώπων Bekker : ἄλλῳ TWF : ἀνθρωπίνῳ Syndenham : ἀνθρωπείῳ
Heindorf

Bekker's ἀνθρώπων γένει restores sense to the nonsensical ἄλλῳ γένει
of the MSS. ἄνθρωπος, one of the so-called *nomina sacra*, was often
abbreviated and this caused the error: ΑΝΩΝ→ΑΛΛΩΙ. The phrase
ἀνθρώπων γένος is strongly confirmed by the corresponding expressions παρθένων γένος (289A5, 9) and θεῶν γένος (289A9, B6–7), and
especially by the strict balance of this sentence:

(1) πιθήκων ὁ κάλλιστος = χυτρῶν ἡ καλλίστη
(2) αἰσχρός = αἰσχρά
(3) ἀνθρώπων γένει = παρθένων γένει
(4) συμβάλλειν = συμβάλλειν.

Syndenham's ἀνθρωπίνῳ, therefore, and Heindorf's ἀνθρωπείῳ both
are much less likely to be right (despite 289C8 τὸ ἀνθρώπειον γένος);
they are, in fact, illustrations of the reluctance of scholars to deviate
from the reading of the MSS—which in this case happened to be a
dative case.

A few scholars (Bywater, Zilles, Heidel) would retain ἄλλῳ γένει,
comparing Plotinus 6.3.11: καίτοι καὶ καλὸν λεγόμενον φανείη ἂν
πρὸς ἄλλο αἰσχρόν, οἷον ἀνθρώπου κάλλος πρὸς θεῶν· πιθήκων,
φησίν, ὁ κάλλιστος αἰσχρὸς συμβάλλειν ἑτέρῳ γένει. This passage
proves not that ἄλλῳ γένει is sound, but that it is a very old corruption.

§53

A very instructive specimen of an ancient corruption is furnished by
fragment 118 (Diels–Kranz) of Heraclitus. This fragment, written in

§53. An Early Corruption of Heraclitus

Heraclitus' typically oracular style, is quoted by Stobaeus (*Florilegium* 5.8) in the following form:

αὔη ξηρὴ ψυχὴ σοφωτάτη καὶ ἀρίστη.

Stephanus deleted ξηρὴ as an explanatory gloss on the rather uncommon adjective αὔη. This seems to me correct, and I agree with those (e.g. Bywater, Burnet, Kranz) who believe that Heraclitus wrote αὔη ψυχὴ σοφωτάτη καὶ ἀρίστη. Compare fragment 117, where the contrary expression ὑγρὴν τὴν ψυχήν occurs. Once ξηρὴ had intruded itself, the words became liable to further corruption. As this *dictum* was often quoted in antiquity, we can still trace the vagaries it underwent (for exact references, see *Vorsokr.*[9] 1.177, where they are conveniently listed). The simplest type of corruption may be seen in Porphyry, Synesius, and Eustathius, where αὔη disappears and is supplanted by ξηρὴ. More serious is the altered form of the sentence as it appears in Musonius, Plutarch, Galen, and Hermias of Alexandria: αὐγὴ ξηρὴ ψυχὴ σοφωτάτη καὶ ἀρίστη. Here αὔη has become by conjecture αὐγή. (In several passages in Plutarch the MSS give αὔτη; this is a later scribal error for αὐγή. That Plutarch wrote αὐγὴ is shown both by his *De Esu Carn.* 1.6, p. 995E, where αὐγὴ is preserved in the MSS, and more importantly by his *Romulus* 28, where the context proves that he wrote αὐγή. The passage runs as follows: αὐγὴ (αὔτη MSS) γὰρ ψυχὴ ξηρὴ καὶ ἀρίστη, καθ' Ἡράκλειτον, ὥσπερ ἀστραπὴ νέφους διαπταμένη τοῦ σώματος κτλ. For αὐγή used of lightning, see *Iliad* 13.244 and Sophocles *Philoctetes* 1199.) Finally, Philo (*ap.* Eusebius *PE* 8.14, p. 399) preserves a version of the dictum where αὐγὴ itself has suffered a further corruption: οὗ γῆ ξηρή, ψυχὴ σοφωτάτη καὶ ἀρίστη. (οὗ γῆ, however, is not certain; the Greek MSS have αὐγὴ. Editors who print in the Philo fragment οὗ γῆ—which suits the context—do so because of the Armenian version which Aucher here rendered into Latin *in terra sicca animus est sapiens ac virtutem amans*. Wendland, on page 120 of the monograph referred to immediately below, writes "Dass Philo wirklich οὗ γῆ las, ist nicht sicher; die Hss. des Eus. und der Arm. haben manchen Korruptelen gemeinsam wie Prokop und der Arm.") Wendland (*Philos Schrift über die Vorsehung*, p. 81 n. 4) plausibly suggests that all the later quotations of this fragment ultimately go back to Panaetius (and Posidonius), who knew it in a form in which the interpolation ξηρὴ was already present. This would explain why ξηρὴ (or ξηρὰ) is found in all the citations.

Diels came to believe that the original form of the *dictum* was in fact αὐγὴ ξηρὴ ψυχὴ σοφωτάτη καὶ ἀρίστη; Jaeger apparently agreed with him, for in his *Theology of the Early Greek Philosophers*, p. 111, he translates the fragment "Dry flash—wisest and best soul." Possibly they are correct. What is important for us to understand is that Heraclitus' pronouncement suffered some kind of corruption at a very early date with the result that it gained currency among the ancients in two distinct forms:

(1) "Dry ray—wisest and best soul"
(2) "Dry soul—wisest and best."

Both basic versions (with minor variations) are quoted not a few times. This being the case, Walther Kranz, editor of the ninth edition of Diels' *Fragmente der Vorsokratiker*, seems to me to have found the happiest solution to the problem of editing this fragment by printing it as follows:

αὐγὴ ξηρὴ ψυχὴ σοφωτάτη καὶ ἀρίστη oder vielmehr: αὔη ψυχὴ σοφωτάτη καὶ ἀρίστη.

I am indebted for my treatment of this fragment not only to Kranz but to John Burnet, *Early Greek Philosophy*[4], p. 138 n. 2. See also Hense's observations in his edition of the *Reliquiae* of Musonius Rufus, p. 96.9 *app. crit.*, and Mueller, *praef.*, pp. XLIII–XLIV of volume 2 of the *Scripta Minora* of Galen (Teubner edition). Bywater, *Heracliti Ephesii Reliquiae*, pp. 30–31, prints all the passages where this fragment in its different forms is preserved.

§54. Plato *Timaeus* 70A–B

... τὴν δὲ δὴ καρδίαν ἅμμα τῶν φλεβῶν καὶ πηγὴν τοῦ περιφερομένου κατὰ πάντα τὰ μέλη σφοδρῶς αἵματος εἰς τὴν δορυφορικὴν οἴκησιν κατέστησαν ...

ἅμμα APY : ἅμα FW Galenus : ἀρχὴν ἅμα recc. : ἄναμμα "Longinus"

For the meaning of this passage see the full discussion in A. E. Taylor's admirable *Commentary on Plato's Timaeus*. The correct lection is ἄμμα τῶν φλεβῶν, which has been preserved in some good MSS (APY); Plato calls the heart the "knot" or "junction" of the blood vessels because, as Taylor observes, they all meet there. (φλέβες in Plato's day included both veins and arteries; it is often stated that they were first distinguished by Praxagoras [*floruit* 300 B.C.], but see now F. Steckerl, *The Fragments of Praxagoras of Cos and His School*, p. 17 n. 1.) Lindau conjectured νᾶμα, "quod et re ipsa commendatur, et statim sequenti voce πηγήν. Cf. Fragm. Tim. Locr., p. 102A. τροφὰ δὲ πᾶσα, ἀπὸ ῥίζας μὲν τᾶς καρδίας, παγᾶς δὲ τᾶς κοιλίας, ἐπάγεται τῷ σώματι." νᾶμα is a good Platonic word and indeed occurs elsewhere in the *Timaeus* (75E, 77C, 80D), but a consideration of its meaning rules it out of court here. Strictly, νᾶμα (compare νάω) signifies "that which flows," "stream," "running water"; it is *not* a synonym for πηγή (*fons*) a word which is often coupled with ἀρχή. To call the heart the "stream" of the blood vessels is nonsense.

The corruption of ἄμμα to ἅμα, seen in F and W, had already occurred in antiquity, for Galen in his *De Placitis Hippocratis et Platonis* quotes this passage three times in the form τὴν δὲ δὴ καρδίαν ἅμα τῶν φλεβῶν καὶ πηγὴν κτλ. (6.292, 575, 581 Kühn). ἅμα is certainly corrupt here for the very good reason that this version of the citation is untranslatable. It is quite possible that ἄμμα was vitiated to ἅμα *independently* more than once in the MSS; the slip is easy enough. But the fact that in three distinct passages of Galen the lection ἅμα is found is most probably to be explained by assuming that Galen had ἅμα in his own copy of the *Timaeus: non est ponenda pluralitas sine necessitate.* This is evidence that the error is ancient and not merely medieval. That Galen could quote and comment upon words that are clearly corrupt is nothing incredible —nor indeed unusual. There are parallels aplenty for this in the Greek and Roman writers. They had to make do with the MSS available to them just as we have to, and often enough they were unequal to the task. Let it here suffice to call attention to this same Galen floundering before a passage in this same work. See his comments on *Timaeus* 77C4 (*CMG* suppl. 1, p. 13.3–7 Schröder), where, faced with two MS variants, he rejects them both and introduces an impossible conjecture of his own. Pasquali discusses the passage in his *Storia della Tradizione e Critica del Testo*², pp. 266–267. [A word of caution: for our passage, *Timaeus* 70A7 sq., Kühn's edition of Galen is misleading; at 6.575 and 581 he prints τὴν δὲ δὴ καρδίαν ἅμα τῶν φλεβῶν πηγὴν καὶ κτλ. This inversion of καὶ πηγὴν restores grammar to the passage, but it has no MS authority; it is nothing but an unsatisfactory modern conjecture.]

ἀρχὴν ἅμα of some later MSS is a Renaissance conjecture. Taylor suggests that it was "helped by the fact that Aristotle repeatedly calls the heart ἀρχὴ τῶν φλεβῶν." (See, for example, *PA* 665b15, ἡ δὲ καρδία τῶν φλεβῶν ἀρχή; *PA* 665b34, δῆλον ὅτι μόριον καὶ ἀρχὴ τῶν φλεβῶν ἐστιν ἡ καρδία; *HA* 513a21–22, αὗται δ᾽ [αἱ φλέβες] ἔχουσι τὰς ἀρχὰς ἀπὸ τῆς καρδίας.) This may well have been the case, but even without such help the context alone could have prompted the addition of ἀρχὴν and, as noted above, πηγή and ἀρχή tended to be used together. Compare the famous passage in the *Phaedrus* (245C8–9) where we find ... ἀλλὰ καὶ τοῖς ἄλλοις ὅσα κινεῖται τοῦτο πηγὴ καὶ ἀρχὴ κινήσεως.

"Longinus," περὶ ὕψους 32.5, paraphrases this *Timaeus* passage; the relevant part goes as follows: ἄναμμα δὲ [sc. ὁ Πλάτων φησὶ] τῶν φλεβῶν τὴν καρδίαν καὶ πηγὴν τοῦ περιφερομένου σφοδρῶς αἵματος, εἰς τὴν δορυφορικὴν οἴκησιν κατατεταγμένην. ἄναμμα elsewhere means "something which has been enkindled," "an ignited mass"; etymologically the word could mean "an attached knot" and make sense here. The combined evidence, however, of the Plato MSS and Galen exposes it as a corruption—but an important corruption in that it has preserved traces of the genuine ἅμμα. All the extant MSS of "Longinus" are thought to derive from codex Parisinus 2036 (= P) of the tenth century, and it is possible that ἄναμμα is a corruption that occurred in the medieval transmission of "Longinus." There is, however, a piece of evidence which makes it probable that ἄναμμα is rather an ancient corruption known to (or made by) the author of περὶ ὕψους. In the original *Timaeus* passage ἅμμα is preceded by καρδίαν and ἄναμμα looks suspiciously like the product of a dittography: the αν of καρδίαν was attached to ἅμμα. In the "Longinus" citation,

Plato's words have been rearranged so that there is no longer any apparent reason for ἅμμα to corrupt into ἄναμμα *specifically within the MS tradition of the* περὶ ὕψους.

§55. Nemesius Emesenus *De Natura Hominis* 2 (Migne, *PG* 40.537A-B)

... Ἀριστοτέλης δὲ [sc. τὴν ψυχὴν λέγει] ἐντελέχειαν πρώ-
την σώματος φυσικοῦ, ὀργανικοῦ, δυνάμει ζωὴν ἔχοντος· Δείναρχος δὲ ἁρμονίαν τῶν τεσσάρων στοιχείων, ἀντὶ τοῦ κρᾶσιν
καὶ συμφωνίαν τῶν στοιχείων ... δῆλον δὲ ὅτι καὶ τούτων οἱ
μὲν ἄλλοι τὴν ψυχὴν οὐσίαν εἶναι λέγουσιν· Ἀριστοτέλης δὲ
καὶ Δείναρχος ἀνούσιον ...

Dinarchus, the last in the canon of the "ten Attic orators," has no business in a philosophical doxography; Δείναρχος, as Matthaei pointed out in his edition of Nemesius (p. 68), is a mistake for Δικαίαρχος. Dicaearchus, the distinguished student of Aristotle, was a prolific writer, among whose (lost) works was a dialogue περὶ ψυχῆς. There can be no doubt that the views presented here were those of Dicaearchus, not Dinarchus; this is stated explicitly in the so-called *Placita Philosophorum* of Aetius (i.e. pseudo-Plutarch and Stobaeus), 4.2.7: Δικαίαρχος ἁρμονίαν τῶν τεσσάρων στοιχείων (p. 387.5-6 Diels). Theodoretus, the bishop of Cyrus and distinguished exegete of the Antiochene school of theology (died c. 466), in his *Graecorum Affectionum Curatio* 5.18 gives Κλέαρχος δὲ τῶν τεσσάρων εἶναι στοιχείων τὴν ἁρμονίαν. Theodoretus is here going back to the same doxographic source, but whether Κλέαρχος is a corruption which he found in his authority or is to be ascribed to later copyists in the direct MS tradition of Theodoretus himself is not clear. In the case of Nemesius, however, we can be quite certain that he actually wrote Δείναρχος, for he repeats the same mistake below, p. 552A: ἐπεὶ δὲ καὶ Δείναρχος ἁρμονίαν ὡρίσατο τὴν ψυχὴν κτλ. Furthermore, Meletius Monachus in his work

66

De Natura Hominis writes Δείναρχος δὲ ἁρμονίαν ὡρίσατο τὴν ψυχὴν εἶναι (*PG* 64.1292D); Meletius' chief source is Nemesius, and he is unquestionably borrowing here directly from Nemesius. The MSS of both authors uniformly give Δείναρχος (with, of course, the normal orthographic variants Διν- and Δην-); Matthaei was therefore wrong in "correcting" the text of Nemesius to Δικαίαρχος. The confusion occurred in some branch of the doxographic tradition *prior to* Nemesius (whose *floruit* is A.D. 400) and was continued after him by Meletius (ninth century?).

Proper names of similar appearance and/or sound are often interchanged in MSS; in particular, well-known names tend to replace less familiar ones while non-Greek names are especially liable to corruption (the Indian and Persian personal and place names in, say, Arrian can be an editor's despair, as they no doubt were to copyists). Instances of such confusions, needless to say, are legion. In the spurious *Alcibiades* I, p. 105D, Socrates addresses Alcibiades as ὦ φίλε παῖ Κλεινίου καὶ Δεινομάχης. The variant Δεινομένης is well attested in the MSS and the neo-Platonist commentator Proclus knew it, but it can only be a mistake. Below in this same dialogue (123C) Alcibiades is correctly called ὁ Δεινομάχης υἱός without any variants; the name was so well known that the Roman poet Persius could allusively write in one of his satires: *Dinomaches ego sum*. In the *Memorabilia* of Xenophon (1.2.48) a list of Socrates' companions is given: ἀλλὰ Κρίτων τε Σωκράτους ἦν ὁμιλητὴς καὶ Χαιρεφῶν καὶ Χαιρεκράτης καὶ †Ἑρμοκράτης† καὶ Σιμίας καὶ Κέβης καὶ Φαιδώνδας καὶ ἄλλοι ... All the MSS give Ἑρμοκράτης, a perfectly good Greek name; however, it seems out of place among these well-known names, for no Hermocrates is elsewhere mentioned as a friend of Socrates. Van Prinsterer conjectured Ἑρμογένης, which is surely correct. Hermogenes was one of the closest friends of Socrates and was present at his death (*Phaedo* 59B); he was one of the speakers in the *Cratylus*, and Xenophon mentions him often (*Mem.* 2.10.3; 4.8.4; *Symp.* 1.3; 3.8, 14; 4.46 sq.; 6.1 sq.). Dindorf in his edition of the *Memorabilia* correctly explains the cause of corruption; Ἑρμοκράτης was written under the influence of the preceding Χαιρεκράτης. In Plutarch's *De Iside et Osiride* 27 (p. 361F) the transmitted text is οὐ γὰρ ἄλλον εἶναι Σάραπιν ἢ τὸν Πλούτωνά φασι, καὶ ᾽Ἶσιν τὴν Περσέφασσαν, ὡς ᾽Αρχέμαχος εἴρηκεν ὁ Εὐβοεύς, καὶ ὁ Ποντικὸς †῾Ηράκλειτος† τὸ χρηστήριον ἐν Κανώβῳ Πλούτωνος ἡγούμενος εἶναι. Heraclitus of Pontus is unknown, but the great pre-Socratic philosopher of Ephesus had made the name Heraclitus familiar; indeed Plutarch quotes him in the very next chapter (p. 362A, where he is called ῾Ηράκλειτος ὁ φυσικός). Xylander restored ῾Ηρακλείδης here. Heraclides Ponticus was a distinguished authority, famous in antiquity for his dialogues; his interest in things occult is well attested.

When the proper name in question is rare or unknown, the problem becomes especially difficult. The celebrated story in Herodotus (6.105–106) of the Athenian long-distance runner sent to ask for Spartan aid against the Persians who had landed at Marathon is a case in point. Was his name Φιλιππίδης or Φειδιππίδης? How and Wells state in their *Commentary on Herodotus* "Φιλιππίδης, though only found in the second family of MSS, is supported by the other authorities (Paus. i.28.4, viii.54–56; Plut. Herod. Malign. 26, etc. [Add Clem. Alex. *Protr.* 3.44.3]), and almost certainly right. It is a common Athenian name (C.I.A.), whereas Pheidippides is a witticism of Aristophanes (Nub. 67), which he would hardly have dared to make had the name been consecrated in the tale of Marathon." Legrand in his Budé edition of Book 6 writes "Pheidippidès est une variante inspirée des Nuées; un scribe a pu juger que ce nom, composé de φείδω, convenait à un coureur à pied, qui permettait d'économiser les chevaux." Here is the passage from *Nubes* 63–67:

> ἢ μὲν γὰρ ἵππον προσετίθει πρὸς τοὔνομα,
> Ξάνθιππον ἢ Χάριππον ἢ Καλλιπίδην,
> ἐγὼ δὲ τοῦ πάππου 'τιθέμην Φειδωνίδην.
> τέως μὲν οὖν ἐκρινόμεθ'· εἶτα τῷ χρόνῳ
> κοινῇ ξυνέβημεν κάθεμεθα Φειδιππίδην.

The jest has more point, perhaps, if Pheidippides is an outlandish name, but it is still a jest without this. It is idle to talk of witticisms which Aristophanes would "hardly have dared to make"; he would have used any name that pleased his fancy (and the pomposity of choosing a name "consecrated in the tale of Marathon," if anything, would add to the humor). It is equally idle to conjure up a scribe in possession of so remarkable a mixture of learning and lunacy as to correct Herodotus on the basis of this passage of Aristophanes. The facts are as follows. Whichever lection is the true one, the corruption is due to nothing more than a mechanical confusion of uncial Δ and Λ (aided by the fact that ι and ει came to be pronounced identically). In support of Φιλιππίδης are the two points which How and Wells stress: (1) the other ancient authorities cite it, and (2) it is a common Athenian name. Furthermore, the Aristophanes passage *may* show that Φειδιππίδης was an invented name, not in actual usage (the name occurs nowhere else, but Φείδιππος is as old as Homer, *Iliad* 2.678). Φειδιππίδης, on the other hand, is supported by the better Herodotus MSS; it is, moreover, the *lectio difficilior*, since the common name Φιλιππίδης is more likely to have replaced Φειδιππίδης than the reverse. (If Φειδιππίδης is a corruption, it happened early enough for it to be taken over into Latin, since Nepos *Miltiades* 4.3 gives *Phidippus*.) Were I editing Herodotus, I should probably print Φιλιππίδης, and record Φειδιππίδης in the *apparatus* with the query "*an recte?*" Instances such as this one, where certainty is simply not possible, are easily multiplied; in the *Martyrium Polycarpi*, the oldest extant formal account of a Christian martyrdom, chapter 20 begins ὑμεῖς μὲν οὖν ἠξιώσατε διὰ πλειόνων δηλωθῆναι ὑμῖν τὰ γενόμενα, ἡμεῖς δὲ κατὰ τὸ παρὸν ἐπὶ κεφαλαίῳ μεμηνύκαμεν διὰ τοῦ ἀδελφοῦ ἡμῶν Μαρκίωνος. This Marcion is otherwise unknown; the reading Μαρκίωνος, which most editors print, is the reading of *m* (= codex Mosquensis 159), generally regarded as the best MS. The other MSS (*b h p*) read Μάρκου and the Latin version has *Marcianum*, which is evidence for a variant Μαρκιανοῦ. This latter reading (Μαρκιανοῦ) is printed by Lightfoot. Polycarp opposed the prominent Gnostic Marcion (see the story related by Irenaeus *Haer.* 3.3.4); a copyist who knew this could have (a) *unconsciously* written Μαρκίωνος by mental association, thus ejecting the true reading, or (b) *consciously* "corrected" a genuine Μαρκίωνος to Μάρκου (or Μαρκιανοῦ) on the false assumption that Marcion here was a reference to the Gnostic, which could not be right. (Lake in his edition of the

Apostolic Fathers prints Μαρκίωνος and comments: "Not of course to be identified with the famous heretic. If Marcianus be the right text, it is noteworthy that Irenaeus [a disciple of Polycarp] sent his treatise on 'The Apostolic Preaching' to a certain Marcianus. But this was probably forty years later than Polycarp's death.") The above line of reasoning may be examined in more detail. Presumably, the typical Byzantine copyist would not be familiar with the early heretic Marcion, and hence any change of the text due to a mental association of Polycarp and Marcion, conscious or otherwise, would likely be early. Fortunately the early history of the transmission of the *Martyrium Polycarpi* is preserved in an epilogue; chapter 22 reads in part: ταῦτα μετεγράψατο μὲν Γάϊος ἐκ τῶν Εἰρηναίου, μαθητοῦ τοῦ Πολυκάρπου, ὃς καὶ συνεπολιτεύσατο τῷ Εἰρηναίῳ. ἐγὼ δὲ Σωκράτης ἐν Κορίνθῳ ἐκ τῶν Γαΐου ἀντιγράφων ἔγραψα. ἡ χάρις μετὰ πάντων. Ἐγὼ δὲ πάλιν Πιόνιος ἐκ τοῦ προγεγραμμένου ἔγραψα ἀναζητήσας αὐτά, κατὰ ἀποκάλυψιν φανερώσαντός μοι τοῦ μακαρίου Πολυκάρπου, καθὼς δηλώσω ἐν τῷ καθεξῆς ... The Moscow MS, *m*, has an expanded form of this epilogue. It begins ταῦτα μετεγράψατο μὲν Γάϊος ἐκ τῶν Εἰρηναίου συγγραμμάτων ... and then inserts some information about Irenaeus and Polycarp, *including the story about Marcion and Polycarp alluded to above*: ... συναντήσαντός ποτε τῷ ἁγίῳ Πολυκάρπῳ Μαρκίωνος, ἀφ' οὗ οἱ λεγόμενοι Μαρκιωνισταί, καὶ εἰπόντος· ἐπιγίνωσκε ἡμᾶς, Πολύκαρπε, εἶπεν αὐτὸς τῷ Μαρκίωνι· ἐπιγινώσκω, ἐπιγινώσκω τὸν πρωτότοκον τοῦ Σατανᾶ ... It then goes on ἐκ τούτων οὖν, ὡς προλέλεκται, τῶν τοῦ Εἰρηναίου συγγραμμάτων Γάϊος μετεγράψατο, ἐκ δὲ τῶν Γαΐου ἀντιγράφων Ἰσοκράτης ἐν Κορίνθῳ. ἐγὼ δὲ πάλιν Πιόνιος ἐκ τῶν Ἰσοκράτους ἀντιγράφων ἔγραψα κατὰ ἀποκάλυψιν τοῦ ἁγίου Πολυκάρπου ζητήσας αὐτά ... This longer version shows clear signs of not being the original one: (1) the μέν at the beginning (ταῦτα μετεγράψατο μὲν Γάϊος ...) is left dangling; (2) the two genuine postscriptions ἐγὼ δὲ Σωκράτης ... ἐγὼ δὲ πάλιν Πιόνιος ... are stylistically harmonized by a change to the third person: ... Ἰσοκράτης ἐν Κορίνθῳ. ἐγὼ δὲ πάλιν Πιόνιος; (3) no account of the ἀποκάλυψις in fact follows in our MSS ("probably because the 'Pionian' text was part of a larger Acts of Polycarp"

Lake); accordingly codex *m* deliberately omits the clause καθὼς δη-λώσω ἐν τῷ καθεξῆς. The family to which codex *m* belonged at one time was edited by someone familiar with the relationships between Marcion and Polycarp; the lection Μαρκίωνος is preserved in *m* and only in *m*. Once again, is Μαρκίωνος an unconscious slip caused by mental associations? Possibly; we simply do not know. (We *can* say that in *m* Μαρκίωνος is hardly likely to be a deliberate "correction" based on a garbled notion of the Polycarp–Marcion relationship.) Nor do we know whether ᾽Ισοκράτης of *m* or Σωκράτης of the other MSS is the right name in the epilogue. Both names are very common and the person referred to is unknown. How facilely a proper name can become supplanted is well illustrated by a passage in the *Homeric Hymn to Demeter*, verses 313–317:

> ... Ζεὺς ἐνόησεν ἑῷ τ᾽ ἐφράσσατο θυμῷ.
> †"Ηρην† δὲ πρῶτον χρυσόπτερον ὦρσε καλέσσαι
> Δήμητρ᾽ ἠΰκομον πολυήρατον εἶδος ἔχουσαν.
> ὣς ἔφαθ᾽· ἡ δὲ Ζηνὶ κελαινεφέϊ Κρονίωνι
> πείθετο ...

Hera is not Zeus's messenger, *Iris* is, and Ruhnken's correction ῏Ιριν is certain. Compare *Iliad* 8.397–398:

> Ζεὺς δὲ πατὴρ ῎Ιδηθεν ἐπεὶ ἴδε χώσατ᾽ ἄρ᾽ αἰνῶς,
> ῏Ιριν δ᾽ ὤτρυνε χρυσόπτερον ἀγγελέουσαν ...

The confusion is instantly understandable; not only did mental association play its part (Hera was the wife of Zeus), but ῏Ιριν and "Ηρην were quite indistinguishable in pronunciation to a Byzantine Greek. Conversely, in Aristophanes *Aves* 575, ῏Ιριν δέ γ᾽ "Ομηρος ἔφασκ᾽ ἰκέλην εἶναι τρήρωνι πελείῃ, Bentley conjectured "Ηρην. Scholars are not in agreement here; in *Iliad* 5.778, αἱ δὲ βάτην τρήρωσι πελειάσιν ἴθμαθ᾽ ὁμοῖαι, the reference is to Hera and Athene, whereas in the *Homeric Hymn to Apollo* 114 βὰν δὲ ποσὶ τρήρωσι πελειάσιν ἴθμαθ᾽ ὁμοῖαι, Iris and Eileithyia are the subjects. See Allen and Halliday, *The Homeric Hymns*², p. 218, and Rogers' edition of the *Aves ad loc*.

The convention of beginning proper names with a capital letter is observed in neither uncial nor minuscule Greek MSS. For example, ῙΡΙC in uncials and ἶρις in minuscules may mean either "rainbow" or "Iris," the goddess. This ambiguity affects the interpretation of many passages, where it is not clear whether the writer intended a common noun or a proper name, an appellative or a personification. Often an unequivocal answer cannot be given; the lack of an orthographic distinction allowed the ancient writer to use "half-personifications" with more freedom than his modern counterpart. ["Still, in at least part of our MSS proper names are distinguished by a horizontal stroke." B.E.] The Greeks themselves were aware of these difficulties; the second book of the *Argonautica* of Apollonius of Rhodes begins:

> Ἔνθα δ' ἔσαν σταθμοί τε βοῶν αὐλίς τ' Ἀμύκοιο,
> Βεβρύκων βασιλῆος ἀγήνορος, ὅν ποτε νύμφη
> τίκτε Ποσειδάωνι Γενεθλίῳ εὐνηθεῖσα
> Βιθυνὶς Μελίη ὑπεροπλήέστατον ἀνδρῶν.

The ambiguity of Βιθυνὶς Μελίη is clearly stated by Mooney in his commentary: "Three interpretations have been given: (1) a Bithynian nymph whose name was Melia, (2) a nymph of the class called Meliae (cf. Hes. *Th.* 187) whose name was Bithynis, (3) a Bithynian nymph of the class called Meliae (whose proper name is not given). Of these the first seems the best. Melia, daughter of Oceanus, was mother of Amycus by Poseidon, cf. Hyg. *Fab.* 17, Amycus Neptuni et Melies filius: Serv. *ad Aen.* 5.373." Here are three scholia on this passage (pp. 124–125 Wendel):

(a) Βιθυνὶς Μελίη: ἄδηλον πότερόν ἐστι τὸ κύριον. Μελίαν δέ φησιν αὐτὴν διὰ τό τινας τῶν νυμφῶν Μελίας καλεῖσθαι ἀπὸ Μελίας τῆς Ὠκεανοῦ, ὥς φησι Καλλίμαχος [frag. 598 (404) Pfeiffer], ἢ διὰ τὸ περὶ μελίας δένδρα διατρίβειν καθάπερ Ἀμαδρυάδας· Βιθυνίδα δὲ διὰ τὸ Βιθυνὴν τὸ γένος τυγχάνειν κτλ.

(b) Βιθυνίς: ὄνομα κύριον.

(c) Μελίη: ἐπίθετον.

The *Etymologicum Genuinum* has two derivative entries which refer to this passage:

(a) Βιθυνὶς Μελίη: εἴρηται εἰς τὸ ὑπεροπλήέστατον.

(b) ὑπεροπλήεστατον: . . . ἡ δὲ Μελία ἀμφίβολον, ἢ κύριον
ὄνομα τῆς νύμφης ἢ ἐπίθετον.

Fränkel prints verses 364–367 of this same book of the *Argonautica* as
follows:

> τήνδε περιγνάμψαντι, Πολὺς παρακέκλιται ἤδη
> Αἰγιαλός. Πολέος δ' ἐπὶ πείρασιν Αἰγιαλοῖο
> ἀκτῇ ἐπὶ προβλῆτι ῥοαὶ "Αλυος ποταμοῖο
> δεινὸν ἐρεύγονται.

Schneider first saw that Αἰγιαλός was a proper name here rather than
αἰγιαλός, "beach." (Of course the place name was in origin a descrip-
tive appellative, as often.) H. Faerber (*Zur dichterischen Kunst in Ap. Rh.'
Argon.*, diss. Berlin 1932, p. 102) argued that Πολύς is part of the place
name; he compares 2.944 and the Orphic *Argonautica* verse 737. Αἰγιαλός occurs as a place name also, for example at 1.178 and Homer *Iliad*
2.575, 855. Stephanus of Byzantium s.v. Αἰγιαλός states in part:
. . . ἔστιν ἕτερος Αἰγιαλὸς προσεχὴς τῷ Πόντῳ μετὰ τὴν Κάραμβιν
ἄκραν, ὡς 'Απολλώνιος. In both passages of Book 2 of Apollonius
where Αἰγιαλός seems to be a proper name, Κάραμβις also occurs
(verses 361 and 943). Stephanus' testimony, therefore, supports Αἰγιαλός in Apollonius, but it is negative evidence against Faerber's ingenious Πολὺς Αἰγιαλός. Stephanus, at least, had never heard of any
such place. Similarly to αἰγιαλός, ἀκτή also often became a place
name, as in the case of the promontory Akte in Chalcidice; Actium,
the site of Octavian's famous victory, is in reality the Greek diminu-
tive "Ακτιον, "Little Promontory." Attica, ἡ 'Αττική, was originally,
before the dissimilation of consonants, ἡ 'Ακτική, it too deriving from
ἀκτή. An ambiguity in Theocritus *Idyll* 17.7–11 seems to have escaped
the notice of the editors:

> αὐτὰρ ἐγὼ Πτολεμαῖον ἐπιστάμενος καλὰ εἰπεῖν
> ὑμνήσαιμ'· ὕμνοι δὲ καὶ ἀθανάτων γέρας αὐτῶν.
> "Ιδαν ἐς πολύδενδρον ἀνὴρ ὑλατόμος ἐλθών
> παπταίνει, παρεόντος ἄδην, πόθεν ἄρξεται ἔργου.
> τί πρῶτον καταλέξω; ἐπεὶ πάρα μυρία εἰπεῖν . . .

73

Gow comments at verse 9: "πολύδενδρον: *Il.* 21.449 "Ἴδης ...
πολυπτύχου ὑληέσσης, Suid. "Ἴδη· πᾶν σύμφυτον ὄρος. T. is probably
thinking of the woodcutting scene at *Il.* 23.114ff." At *Iliad* 23.117 we
do indeed read ὅτε δὴ κνημοὺς προσέβαν πολυπίδακος "Ἴδης, but precisely because the woodcutters were in fact on Mount Ida. "Ἴδη was
originally a common noun and the definition given in the *Suda* (Gow's
note, above) is correct. Hesychius s.v. ἴδη gives in part ... ἢ ὄρος
Τροίας. ἢ ὕλη ... δηλοῖ δὲ καὶ τὸν ὑψηλὸν τόπον ... "Ἴωνες δὲ δρυμῶν ὄρος. "Ἴδη as a proper name (used most frequently of the two
mountains respectively in the Troad and on Crete) is very common,
but it is not the original usage. ἴδη as an appellative is used several times
by Herodotus and ἴδαν ἐς πολύδενδρον (for this passage) is recognized
by LSJ s.v. ἴδη. Theocritus may well have particularized to "Ἴδαν
(*which* Mount Ida?) in this "paratactic simile"; poets have an affinity
for the specific. Homer, however, is less precise in his woodcutter
similes: ὁ δ᾽ ἐν κονίῃσι χαμαὶ πέσεν αἴγειρος ὥς, / ἥ ῥά τ᾽ ἐν εἰαμενῇ
ἕλεος μεγάλοιο πεφύκει κτλ. (*Il.* 4.482–483); ἤριπε δ᾽ ὡς ὅτε τις δρῦς
ἤριπεν ἢ ἀχερωΐς, / ἠὲ πίτυς βλωθρή, τήν τ᾽ οὔρεσι τέκτονες ἄνδρες /
ἐξέταμον κτλ. (*Il.* 13.389–391). Theocritus' fellow Alexandrian, Apollonius, adopts a similar general tone in his similes: ὡς δ᾽ ὅτε δούρατα
μακρὰ νέον πελέκεσσι τυπέντα / ὑλοτόμοι στοιχηδὸν ἐπὶ ῥηγμῖνι
βάλωσιν, / ὄφρα νοτισθέντα κρατεροὺς ἀνεχοίατο γόμφους (1.1003–
1005); ἀλλ᾽ ὥς τίς τ᾽ ἐν ὄρεσσι πελωρίη ὑψόθι πεύκη, / τήν τε θοοῖς
πελέκεσσιν ἔθ᾽ ἡμιπλῆγα λιπόντες / ὑλοτόμοι δρυμοῖο κατήλυθον
(4.1682–1684). In Latin, Valerius Flaccus shows the same indefiniteness:
ac veluti magna iuvenum cum densa *securi* / silva *labat eqs.* (*Arg.* 3.163–
164); in Vergil's well-known simile (*Aen.* 2.626 sq.) the expression
used is *summis ... in montibus.* There is a legitimate doubt whether
Theocritus intended "Ἴδαν or ἴδαν. [A possible objection that ἴδη is an
Ionic word because of its occurrence in Herodotus and Hesychius'
"Ἴωνες δὲ δρυμῶν ὄρος (which is nothing but a reference to Herodotus)
is groundless. Philostratus uses the word and, what is more relevant,
Mount Ida on Crete is located in the center of an island which was
early colonized by Dorian speakers. The only reference to Dorians
(Δωριέες τριχάϊκες) in Homer places them specifically on Crete.] Nor

can we exclude the possibility that Theocritus is using the word in a pregnant sense, both meanings being suggested at once. According to Strabo 8.372 ἄργος δὲ καὶ τὸ πεδίον λέγεται παρὰ τοῖς νεωτέροις, παρ' Ὁμήρῳ δ' οὐδ' ἅπαξ. This use of ἄργος occurs in Callimachus frag. 299.2 Pfeiffer, Νηπείης ... ἄργος. The *Electra* of Euripides begins Ὦ γῆς παλαιὸν ἄργος, Ἰνάχου ῥοαί; Murray observes in his *apparatus* "Vulgo post Victorium "Άργος, sed cf. Callim. ap. Schol. Ap. Rhod. 1.1116." Denniston in his edition of the *Electra* comments "ἄργος, with a small alpha, is, I think, sound ... the best parallel is *Ba.* 1043 ἐπεὶ θεράπνας τῆσδε Θηβαίας χθονὸς λιπόντες ..., where θεράπνας is half common, half proper, just as ἄργος is here." See further Dodds at *Bacchae* 1043–1045.

Personifications are especially elusive; in Euripides *Heracleidae* 433–434 Iolaus exclaims:

> οἴμοι· τί δῆτ' ἔτερψας ὦ τάλαινά με
> ἐλπὶς τότ', οὐ μέλλουσα διατελεῖν χάριν;

Here I should prefer Ἐλπίς; the personification is found in Hesiod *Works and Days* 96, Pindar frag. 214 Snell, and Sophocles *OT* 157–158, ὦ χρυσέας τέκνον Ἐλπίδος, / ἄμβροτε Φάμα. Similarly, in *Orestes* 213–214 Murray prints:

> ὦ πότνια Λήθη τῶν κακῶν, ὡς εἶ σοφὴ
> καὶ τοῖσι δυστυχοῦσιν εὐκταία θεός.

Here the poet is clearly "deifying," and Λήθη is better than the λήθη which I have seen printed in some other editions. When Epictetus—or rather Arrian—writes in the *Discourses* 2.20.29 "φαντασία μοι ἐγένετο ἐλαίου ἀδιάκριτος, ὁμοιοτάτη, νὴ τὴν σὴν τύχην," τύχη is at least a quasi-divinity and is probably to be printed Τύχη (see LSJ s.v. τύχη IV.1). These latter examples really involve nothing but a question of orthographic convention, and the sense is little affected whether we capitalize or not. Such is not always the case. See, for instance, Dodds at Euripides *Bacchae* 1024–1026, where he argues against Wilamowitz' δράκοντος ... "Οφεος.

§56

Punctuation in general, and not merely orthographic convention, is often taken for granted by the modern reader, who wants reminding that a printed edition of a classical text in many respects bears little resemblance to its ancient or medieval counterpart. An editor can ill afford to be so casual. "I have paid special attention to the punctuation, a change in which often makes emendation unnecessary." So wrote Sir David Ross in the introduction to his edition of Aristotle's *Metaphysics*. That is the practice of a sound scholar. The ambiguities that can result from imprecise punctuation were of course seen by the Greeks. I need not multiply illustrations; one will do. Euripides *Orestes* 215–216:

> πόθεν ποτ' ἦλθον δεῦρο; πῶς δ' ἀφικόμην;
> ἀμνημονῶ γάρ, τῶν πρὶν ἀπολειφθεὶς φρενῶν.

"Porson places a comma at τῶν πρὶν, but this probably agrees with φρενῶν. So Bacch. 947 τὰς δὲ πρὶν φρένας οὐκ εἶχες ὑγιεῖς." Paley. Add *Andromache* 164, ἀντὶ τῶν πρὶν ὀλβίων φρονημάτων. One scholium on these verses goes as follows: τῶν πρὶν ἀπολειφθεὶς φρενῶν: τῶν πρὶν φρενῶν ἀπολειφθεὶς ἐν τῇ μανίᾳ, οὐχὶ νῦν ἀπολειφθεὶς τῶν φρενῶν ἀμνημονῶ, ἀλλ' ἐν τῇ νόσῳ· τὸ γὰρ ὄργανον, δι' οὗ ἀναφέρομεν τὰ πραττόμενα, συννοσεῖ τῷ σώματι. ἀμνημονῶ τί πέπρακταί μοι ἐν τῇ νόσῳ, τῶν προτέρων φρενῶν ἀπολειφθεὶς καὶ μανείς. Here is another scholium on the same passage: Ἄλλως. τῶν πρίν: ἕως τούτου ὀφείλει στίζειν, εἶτα, ἀπολειφθεὶς φρενῶν. δεῖ δὲ νοεῖν οὐχὶ νῦν ἀπολειφθεὶς τῶν φρενῶν, ἀλλὰ τότε· νῦν γὰρ φρονίμως διαλέγεται. We are not to think that punctuation was a new creation of the Alexandrian grammarians; Rudolf Pfeiffer, the great master in such matters, writes " . . . in fact, some sort of punctuation was indispensable for the Greek *scriptio continua* from the beginning; the hexametric verse graffito of about 700 B.C., found in Ischia, is at the moment the earliest inscription known to me which bears signs of punctuation" (*History of Classical Scholarship* [Oxford 1968] 179). Pfeiffer cites Isocrates *or.* 15.59 for mention of the παραγραφή and Aristotle *Rhetorica* 1409a21 for the same term. He also refers to the well-known passage in the *Rhetorica* (1407b11ff) where Aristotle calls attention to the ambiguous opening words of Heraclitus: τὰ γὰρ Ἡρακλείτου διαστίξαι ἔργον διὰ τὸ ἄδηλον εἶναι ποτέρῳ πρόσκειται, τῷ ὕστερον ἢ τῷ πρότερον, οἷον ἐν τῇ ἀρχῇ αὐτῇ τοῦ συγγράμματος· φησὶ γὰρ "τοῦ λόγου τοῦδ' ἐόντος ἀεὶ ἀξύνετοι ἄνθρωποι γίγνονται." ἄδηλον γὰρ τὸ ἀεί, πρὸς ποτέρῳ ⟨δεῖ⟩ διαστίξαι. Heraclitus' words have proved prophetic, for scholars are still not in agreement here! Another important classical reference (not given by Pfeiffer) is Isocrates *or.* 12.17: ἕως μὲν οὖν τοὺς λόγους ἡμῶν ἐλυμαίνοντο, παραναγιγνώσκοντες ὡς δυνατὸν κάκιστα τοῖς αὐτῶν καὶ διαιροῦντες οὐκ ὀρθῶς καὶ κατακνίζοντες καὶ πάντα τρόπον διαφθείροντες, οὐδὲν ἐφρόντιζον τῶν ἀπαγγελλομένων κτλ. The seventh-century abbot, Anastasius Sinaita, in the proem to his Ὁδηγός (Migne, *PG* 89.36B), makes an appeal to the copyists which in its simplicity has something almost pathetic about it. I have never seen it quoted and so reproduce it here for its intrinsic interest to the question at hand:

Πρὸς τούτοις δυσωποῦμεν τὸν μεταγράφειν μέλλοντα παραθέσθαι καὶ τὰ σχόλια· σημειώσασθαι δὲ ἐπιμελῶς καὶ τοὺς τόνους καὶ στιγμὰς καὶ ὑποστιγμὰς καὶ τὰ σόλοικα. Καὶ γὰρ ἄλλοτέ τινες ἰδιῶται, μεταγράψαντες ἡμῶν δογματικὸν τόμον, ἐξ ἀγνοίας βλασφημιῶν αὐτὸν ἐπλήρωσαν.

§57

Calvert Watkins begins his excellent paper "An Indo-European Construction in Greek and Latin" (*HSCP* 71 [1966] 115–119) with the following statement: "In the course of the last fifty years a number of scholars have independently called attention to a singular syntactic feature of both Greek and Latin: the iteration of a compound verb in a succeeding clause or sentence by the simple verb alone, but with the semantic force of the compound." He then collects all the relevant references and on page 117 remarks: "I have purposefully quoted all

the references cited by these scholars—in all humility, having no further
examples to add from Greek or Latin—since I think it perhaps of some
advantage to have them gathered together in one place." Consulting
the references given by Watkins, one discovers that all the Greek
examples cited are from Attic Greek, especially the drama. A perusal
of Elmsley's note on *Medea* 1219 (= 1252), for example, might give the
impression that the idiom is peculiar to Greek tragedy. R. A. Neil on
Aristophanes *Equites* 98 goes so far as to state explicitly: "This usage is
the Attic counterpart to the Epic epanalepsis of prepositions, where the
verb is omitted." (Watkins, let me hasten to add, was not so deceived;
the whole point of his paper is to demonstrate that this usage is a genuine feature not only of archaic Greek and Latin but of "the common
original language, Indo-European itself." His demonstration of this,
documented, with much learning, from Hittite, is quite successful.) I
purpose here first to list some further Greek examples, including some
non-Attic instances, and then discuss several passages where this syntactic feature has a bearing on the reading:

1. Pindar *Paean* 4.21–23 = frag. 52d Snell διαγινώσκομαι . . .
   γινώσκομαι
2. Aristophanes *Vespae* 1334–1335 προσκαλούμενοι . . . καλού-
   μενοι
3. Euripides *Herakles* 488–489 συνενέγκαιμ' . . . ἐνεγκοῦσ'
4. ——— *Cyclops* 657–659 ἐκκαίετε . . . καιέτω
5. Plato *Apology* 21C διασκοπῶν . . . σκοπῶν
6. ——— *Philebus* 23D προσδεήσει . . . δέῃ
7. ——— *Timaeus* 84E–85A ἐναπολαμβάνεται . . . ἀποληφθέν
8. [Plato] I *Alcibiades* 108B προσπαλαίειν . . . παλαίειν
9. Xenophon *Hellenica* 3.3.9 συλλαβεῖν . . . ληφθέντας
10. ——— *Hiero* 8.2 ἐπισκοποῦντες . . . σκοπῶμεν
11. ——— *Symposium* 5.8 διαφερόντων . . . φερόντων
12. ——— ibid. 6.6 ἐπικαλούμενος . . . ἐκαλούμην
13. "Hippocrates" *Ars* 11 διεξαρκέσῃ . . . ἐξαρκέσει
14. Apollonius Rhodius *Argon.* 1.1280–1282 ὑπολάμπεται . . .
    λάμπεται

78

15. Galenus *UP* 3.619 (Kühn) ἀναψύχειν ... ἐκθερμαίνεσθαι ...
    ψύχειν ... θερμαίνειν
16. Arrianus *Anabasis* 1.17.1 ἀποφέρειν ... ἔφερον
17. ——— *ibid.* 5.4.3 ἐκφέρει ... φέρουσιν
18. ——— *ibid.* 6.17.5–6 ἐπεργαζομένων ... ἐργάζεσθαι
19. ——— *ibid.* 7.3.2 ἐπιφέροντας ... ἔφερον
20. ——— *Indica* 34.4 προελθόντες ... ἐλθόντες
21. Diogenes Laertius 10.28 ἐκθέσθαι ... παραθέμενος ... θήσο-
    μεν (it is not clear to me which compound is taken up by
    θήσομεν; see the passage).

It appears, I may note, from these examples that this phenomenon is
not affected by a change of voice in the verb and that it may occur even
when the compound verb has *two* prefixes. For the latter, see the list
given above, numbers 7 and 13, where the first of two prefixes is
omitted in the iterated verb. In Plato *Symposium* 211B–C there seems
to be a case where the simplex carries the full force of a double compound: ἐπανιών ... ἰέναι ... ἐπανιέναι; see the context. It has not
been observed that sometimes a writer returns to the compound after
using the simplex; so Plato here, and possibly Xenophon *Hellenica*
5.4.54: παρακολουθούντων ... ἠκολούθει ... παρηκολούθουν [†καθά-
περ† ἠκολούθουν MSS: καθὰ παρηκολούθουν Renehan; see *HSCP* 67
(1963) 271–272].

The following passage comes from the third book of Epictetus' *Discourses* (3.9.22):

τοῖς ‹παιδίοις› εἰς στενόβρογχον κεράμιον καθιεῖσιν τὴν χεῖρα
καὶ ἐκφέρουσιν ἰσχαδοκάρυα ταὐτὸ συμβαίνει· ἂν πληρώσῃ τὴν
χεῖρα, ἐξενεγκεῖν οὐ δύναται, εἶτα κλάει. ἄφες ὀλίγα ἐξ αὐτῶν
καὶ ἐξοίσεις. καὶ σὺ ἄφες τὴν ὄρεξιν· μὴ πολλῶν ἐπιθύμει καὶ
οἴσεις.

παιδίοις add. Wolf   ταὐτὸ Capps : τοῦτο

Oldfather renders the last sentence: "And so do you too drop your
desire; do not set your heart upon many things and you will obtain"(?).
In a note on the last word of the Greek, οἴσεις, he comments: "Wolf

plausibly suggested εὐροήσεις, 'you will prosper,' for this extremely abrupt and obscure locution." The locution is not abrupt nor is it obscure. Epictetus is keeping up the metaphor of the στενόβρογχον κεράμιον; οἴσεις is clearly being used in the sense of the compound ἐξοίσεις, which has just been used (preceded, be it noted, by ἐκφέρουσιν and ἐξενεγκεῖν).

Arrian *Anabasis* 5.3.1–2

καὶ ταῦτα ὅπως τις ἐθέλει ὑπολαβὼν ἀπιστείτω ἢ πιστευέτω. οὐ γὰρ ἔγωγε Ἐρατοσθένει τῷ Κυρηναίῳ πάντη ξυμφέρομαι, ὃς λέγει πάντα ὅσα ἐς τὸ θεῖον ἀναφέρεται ἐκ Μακεδόνων πρὸς χάριν τὴν Ἀλεξάνδρου ἐς τὸ ὑπέρογκον ἐπιφημισθῆναι. καὶ γὰρ καὶ σπήλαιον λέγει ἰδόντας ἐν Παραπαμισάδαις τοὺς Μακεδόνας . . . φημίσαι, ὅτι τοῦτο ἄρα ἦν τοῦ Προμηθέως τὸ ἄντρον ἵνα ἐδέδετο κτλ.

For ἐπιφημισθῆναι there is in some MSS a variant reading ἐπευφημηθῆναι; Lobeck in his *Phrynichus*, p. 597, rightly defends ἐπιφημισθῆναι. To his arguments may be added the fact that the simple verb φημίσαι occurs in the next sentence; it is an iteration not of ἐπευφημηθῆναι but of ἐπιφημισθῆναι. That Arrian is fond of this syntactic practice is adequately documented in my list of examples given above.

[Aristotle] *Problemata* 868b34–869a12

Διὰ τί οἱ ἀγωνιῶντες ἱδροῦσι τοὺς πόδας, τὸ δὲ πρόσωπον οὔ; . . . ἢ ὅτι καὶ ἡ ἀγωνία ἐστὶ θερμότητος οὐ μετάστασις ὥσπερ ἐν τῷ φόβῳ ἐκ τῶν ἄνω τόπων εἰς τοὺς κάτω . . . ἀλλ' αὔξησις θερμοῦ, ὥσπερ ἐν τῷ θυμῷ· καὶ γὰρ ὁ θυμὸς ζέσις τοῦ θερμοῦ ἐστι τοῦ περὶ τὴν καρδίαν· καὶ ὁ ἀγωνιῶν οὐ διὰ φόβον καὶ διὰ ψύξιν [a 7] πάσχει, ἀλλὰ διὰ τὸ μέλλον.

Διὰ τί τὸ πρόσωπον ἐξέρυθροι γίνονται, οὐχ ἱδροῦσι δέ; ἢ διὰ τὸ μᾶλλον θερμαίνεσθαι, ὥστε τὸ μὲν ἐν τῷ προσώπῳ ὑγρὸν ξηραίνει ἡ θερμότης ἐπιπολάζουσα, τὸ δὲ ἐν τοῖς ποσὶ συντήκει κτλ.

(I have given the text as printed by the Teubner editors Ruelle, Knoellinger, and Klek.) The solution proposed for the first πρόβλημα is a *physiological* one (ἡ ἀγωνία ἐστὶ . . . αὔξησις θερμοῦ). The explanation διὰ τὸ μέλλον (a7), "because of what is going to happen," is not. Again, it is explicitly stated that the reason is *not* a μετάστασις θερμότητος, ὥσπερ ἐν τῷ φόβῳ; it must therefore contrast with what takes place ἐν τῷ φόβῳ. Fear, according to Aristotle, (*EN* 1115a9), is a προσδοκία κακοῦ (cf. Plato *Prot.* 358D; *SVF*, Index s.v. φόβος); it is difficult to discern much of a contrast between προσδοκία κακοῦ and the implications of διὰ τὸ μέλλον. The main, though not exclusive, source for the *Problemata* was the Theophrastean Corpus and by chance the very passage of Theophrastus which was excerpted here is still extant. It occurs in the treatise *De Sudoribus* (frag. 9.36= 3.147 Wimmer); the correct reading may be recovered from the corresponding sentence in Theophrastus which goes καὶ ⟨οἱ?⟩ ἀγωνιῶντες δὲ οὐ διὰ φόβον τοῦτο πάσχουσιν ἀλλὰ διὰ τὸ μᾶλλον ἐκθερμαίνεσθαι. In the *Problemata* passage ἐκθερμαίνεσθαι fell out for some reason; this left the meaningless διὰ τὸ μᾶλλον. μᾶλλον was then changed by conjecture to μέλλον in an attempt to make some sense of the words. Read διὰ τὸ μᾶλλον ⟨ἐκθερμαίνεσθαι⟩; this phrase, it should be noted, is an exact synonym for αὔξησις θερμοῦ, the reason just mentioned as the cause of ἀγωνία. That the compiler, like Theophrastus, gave a physiological explanation, is further confirmed by the explanatory (physiological) addition καὶ διὰ ψύξιν, after διὰ φόβον (for φόβος is a κατάψυξις *Probl.* 869b7); these two words are not in Theophrastus. In the next πρόβλημα the compiler (869a10) writes διὰ τὸ μᾶλλον θερμαίνεσθαι; at first glance this seems to support E. S. Forster, who in *CQ* 27 (1933) 141 conjectured διὰ τὸ μᾶλλον ⟨θερμαίνεσθαι⟩ at 869a7. But my conjecture ⟨ἐκθερμαίνεσθαι⟩ (made without knowledge of Forster's proposal) is surely confirmed by the Theophrastean original, which shows only ἐκθερμαίνεσθαι. Why then θερμαίνεσθαι two lines below? It is one more instance of the iteration of the *compositum* by the *simplex* (I owe this acute observation to Professor Charles Murgia). For an example, in a similar (i.e. physiological) context, of ἐκθερμαίνω continued by θερμαίνω, see Galen *De Usu Partium* 8.2 (3.619 Kühn= 1.449 Helmreich): καίτοι κἂν εἰ περιέχοιτο μόνον [sc. ὁ ἐγκέφαλος], οὐ δήπου τὴν μὲν καρδίαν αὐτὸς ἱκανὸς ἦν ἀναψύχειν, οὕτω μὲν πόρρω διωκι-

§57. Compound and Simplex Verbs

σμένος, διττοῖς δ' ὀστῶν διαφράγμασι διειργόμενος, ὑπὸ δὲ τῆς μήνιγγος οὐκ ἂν ἤμελλεν ἐκθερμαίνεσθαι διὰ παντὸς ὁμιλούσης ἐν χρῷ, εἰ μή τι τὸ μὲν ψυχρὸν μόριον ψύχειν πάντα καὶ τὰ μὴ πλησιάζοντα δύναται, τὸ θερμὸν δ' οὐδὲ τὰ πλησιάζοντα θερμαίνειν ἱκανόν ἐστιν. [This discussion of *Problemata* 868b34 sq. is a somewhat revised condensation of my treatment of the passage in my paper "Aristotle's Definition of Anger," *Philologus* 107 (1963) 70–72.]

Theognis 1349–1350

οὕτω μὴ θαύμαζε, Σιμωνίδη, οὕνεκα κἀγώ
ἐξεδάμην καλοῦ παιδὸς ἔρωτι δαμείς.

So read our MSS and so prints the most recent editor of Theognis, Douglas Young. A redundancy such as ἐξεδάμην . . . δαμείς is quite uncharacteristic of Greek poetry. What Theognis actually wrote was ἐξεφάνην . . . δαμείς; the conjecture occurred independently to Bergk, Baiter, Ahrens, and myself—a fact which shows that the correction was both easy and obvious. ἐξεφάνην is supported by verses 1341–1344:

Αἰαῖ, παιδὸς ἐρῶ ἀπαλόχροος, ὅς με φίλοισιν
πᾶσι μάλ᾽ ἐκφαίνει κοὐκ ἐθέλοντος ἐμοῦ.
Τλήσομαι οὐ κρύψας ἀεκούσι⟨α⟩ πολλὰ βίαια·
οὐ γὰρ ἐπ᾽ αἰκελίῳ παιδὶ δαμεὶς ἐφάνην.

In verse 1344 ἐφάνην is used in the sense of the compound ἐξεφάνην; the simple verb is an iteration of ἐκφαίνει in verse 1342, so that δαμεὶς ἐφάνην is exactly parallel to ἐξεφάνην . . . δαμείς. The error is to be explained from the common scribal practice of copying poetry *a verse at a time*. In verse 1350 the last word the scribe said to himself was δαμείς; he then began to write out the verse. With the δαμ of δαμείς still ringing in his ear he unconsciously miswrote ἐξεφάνην as ἐξεδάμην. [See *CP* 60 (1965) 135.]

E. B. Clapp, reviewing Schroeder's 1908 Teubner edition of Pindar in *CP* 4 (1909) 463–465, closed his review with the following suggestion: "No edition of Pindar seems to have observed the close relation, both in subject-matter and rhythm, between Fr. 227 and Fr. 172. It seems probable that Clement of Alexandria, and the Scholiast to Euripides, have here cited successive portions of the same poem. If so, we have, instead of two brief fragments, another considerable passage, as follows:

227   νέων δὲ μέριμναι σὺν πόνοις εἰλισσόμεναι
        δόξαν εὑρίσκοντι· λάμπει δὲ χρόνῳ
        ἔργα μετ᾽ αἰθέρα †λαμπευθέντα†— —

172   οὐ Πηλέος ἀντιθέου μόχθοις νεότας ἐπέλαμψεν μυρίοις;
        πρῶτον μὲν Ἀλκμήνας σὺν υἱῷ Τρώϊον ἂμ πεδίον,
        καὶ μετὰ ζωστῆρας Ἀμαζόνος ἦλθεν, καὶ τὸν Ἰάσονος
                     εὔδοξον πλόον
        ἐκτελέσσαις, εἷλε Μήδειαν ἐν Κόλχων δόμοις."

    227.3 αἰθέρ᾽ ἀερθέντα Boeckh

No editor, to my knowledge, has followed Clapp in printing these two fragments together, but some of them do call attention to his suggestion. Sandys, in his Loeb edition of Pindar, comments significantly on frag. 227: "Professor E. B. Clapp . . . proposes to prefix it to Frag. 172 (158), which is in the same metre, *and has an echo of* λάμπει *in* ἐπέλαμψεν" (my italics). The Greek tendency is to use first the compound and then the simple verb (or else repeat the compound); the supposed "echo" ἐπέλαμψεν would show the reverse order and is in fact an argument against Clapp's collocation of the two fragments. It should be stressed that we are dealing here with *tendencies*, and that the order λάμπει . . . ἐπέλαμψεν is a probable objection to Clapp's proposal, not a certain refutation of it. Watkins (see this sec., *ad init.*), p. 116, does in fact adduce two instances of this inversion: Menander *Dysk.* 818 δίδου, μεταδίδου, and Alexis *Asotodidaskalos* 25 Kock πίνωμεν, ἐμπίνωμεν. He adds: "It will be noted that in both cases the forms are juxtaposed, which was not a necessary condition of the earlier construction." This restriction is too narrow; I have seen instances of the compound following the simplex without strict juxtaposition, though, alas, I have failed to write down the references. The important point is that the compound followed by the simplex is a normal and not infrequent construction; the reverse order is much less common. The only examples that I have at hand of this latter order are Plato *Philebus* 50A6–7: κεραννύντας . . . συγκεραννύναι, and *Symposium* 183B3– 5: δέδοται ὑπὸ τοῦ νόμου ἄνευ ὀνείδους πράττειν, ὡς πάγκαλόν τι πρᾶγμα διαπραττομένου. In this latter passage, however, Plato had already written shortly before διαπράξασθαι (A1) . . . , πράττειν (A8).

"On occasion the prefix of a compound verb is understood with a subsequent simple verb, even though the simple verb be derived from an entirely different root" (Clausen in *AJP* 76 [1955] 50). He was writing of Latin, but added that "this phenomenon appears in Greek, too: Aesch., *Prom.*, 331: πάντων μετασχὼν καὶ τετολμηκὼς ἐμοί . . . Similar also are Soph., *Antig.*, 537: καὶ ξυμμετίσχω καὶ φέρω τῆς αἰτίας and Soph., *O.R.*, 347: καὶ ξυμφυτεῦσαι τοὔργον εἰργάσθαι θ' . . ." There is an instance of this in Plato *Republic* 586A:

> Οἱ ἄρα φρονήσεως καὶ ἀρετῆς ἄπειροι, εὐωχίαις δὲ καὶ τοῖς τοιούτοις ἀεὶ συνόντες, κάτω, ὡς ἔοικεν, καὶ μέχρι πάλιν πρὸς τὸ μεταξὺ φέρονταί τε καὶ ταύτῃ πλανῶνται διὰ βίου, ὑπερβάντες δὲ τοῦτο πρὸς τὸ ἀληθῶς ἄνω οὔτε ἀνέβλεψαν πώποτε οὔτε ἠνέχθησαν κτλ.

The prefix ἀν- is carried over from ἀνέβλεψαν to ἠνέχθησαν, so that this latter verb has the force of ἀνηνέχθησαν. Curiously, "Longinus," who quotes this passage (13.1, with some omissions) cites οὔτ' ἀνέβλεψαν πώποτε οὔτ' ἀνηνέχθησαν. Though accidental omission of the syllable ἀν- before -ην- would be an easy error, we are not to think that the Plato MSS are corrupt. "Longinus," who understood the passage, unintentionally made a very natural misquotation. (In the next chapter, 14.1, he uses this same compound verb again: προσπίπτοντα γὰρ ἡμῖν κατὰ ζῆλον ἐκεῖνα τὰ πρόσωπα καὶ οἷον διαπρέποντα τὰς ψυχὰς ἀνοίσει πως πρὸς τὰ ἀνειδωλοποιούμενα μέτρα.) "Longinus" himself (39.4) has an example of a prefix understood with a verb derived from a different root: ὡς ἔμπαλιν, ἐὰν ἐπεκτείνῃς "παρελθεῖν ἐποίησεν ὥσπερ⟨εἰ⟩ νέφος," τὸ αὐτὸ σημαίνει, οὐ τὸ αὐτὸ δὲ ἔτι προσπίπτει, ὅτι τῷ μήκει τῶν ἄκρων χρόνων συνεκλύεται καὶ διαχαλᾶται τὸ ὕψος τὸ ἀπότομον. As D. A. Russell observes in his commentary (page 175), ". . . we should . . . take συν- as meaning 'with', and indeed assume it with the second verb διαχαλᾶται also ...." That this interpretation is correct seems guaranteed by a sentence toward the beginning of the next chapter (40): ... οὕτως τὰ μεγάλα σκεδασθέντα μὲν ἀπ' ἀλλήλων ἄλλοσ' ἄλλῃ ἅμα ἑαυτοῖς <u>συνδιαφορεῖ καὶ τὸ ὕψος</u>. Indeed, I think that I have detected a second example of the phenomenon in this same chapter, for "Longinus" goes on to use the phrase διὰ μόνου τοῦ συνθεῖναι καὶ ἁρμόσαι ... That ἁρμόσαι is used here in the sense of συναρμόσαι is strongly suggested by a sentence which soon follows: εἰ δ' ἄλλως αὐτὸ συναρμόσεις, φανήσεταί σοι διότι τῆς συνθέσεως ποιητὴς ὁ Εὐριπίδης μᾶλλόν ἐστιν ἢ τοῦ νοῦ. Another instance of συναρμόζειν occurs in 39.3. (The total context of these two chapters, which deal with literary σύνθεσις, should be examined.) By the very nature of this phenomenon, one cannot always determine where it is operative. Plato *Symposium* 219C: ποιήσαντος δὲ δὴ ταῦτα ἐμοῦ οὗτος τοσοῦτον περιεγένετό τε καὶ κατεφρόνησεν καὶ κατεγέλασεν τῆς ἐμῆς ὥρας καὶ ὕβρισεν ... Does ὕβρισεν here have the force of καθύβρισεν? The compound is classical and would be quite apt; see LSJ s.v. καθυβρίζω. On the other hand, the simplex gives a satisfactory sense. I at least cannot decide. (Some may feel that the position of τῆς ἐμῆς ὥρας excludes interpreting ὕβρισεν=καθύβρισεν; the objection seems invalid to me.)

§58. Aeschylus *Agamemnon* 1390–1392

> βάλλει μ' ἐρέμνῃ ψακάδι φοινίας δρόσου,
> χαίρουσαν οὐδὲν ἧσσον ἢ διοσδότῳ
> γάνει σπορητὸς κάλυκος ἐν λοχεύμασιν.

διοσδότῳ γάνει is Porson's famous correction for διὸς νότῳ γᾶν εἰ of the MSS. The resultant sense is perfect and the diction is quite Aeschylean. For διόσδοτος see *Eumenides* 626 and *Septem* 948 (here, for metrical reasons, the form διόδοτος, conjectured by Bothe, is usually printed); for γάνος see *Agamemnon* 579 and *Persae* 483, 615. It is perhaps not accidental that Lycophron (*Alexandra* 1365) uses γάνος absolutely of "water"; for imitations of Aeschylean diction in Lycophron, see below, sec. 78. The origin of the corruption is patent; uncial ΔΙΟCΔΟΤΩ was misread as ΔΙΟCΝΟΤΩ and falsely divided, just as the rare word ΓΑΝΕΙ in the next verse was falsely divided to produce two words recognizable as Greek—to the despite of grammar and sense. Eduard Fraenkel, in his commentary on this play, observes at verse 1391 "The νότωι of the MSS is a corruption of the common type in which two elements are combined, a mechanical error arising from the literal similarity of two words, and a mental error, the writer's thought straying to some word suggested by the context: the rainy wind seemed to fit here." He goes on to give some illuminating examples of this phenomenon; the whole note well repays a perusal.

In recent times two alternate solutions of this passage have been proposed; Lawson conjectured Διὸς νότῳ γαίει, and Lloyd-Jones Διὸς νότῳ γαθεῖ (both had been anticipated by Hermann's γανᾷ). Porson's conjecture seems to me more elegant and probable than either. The repetition of a verb of rejoicing here is unnecessary and slightly prosaic (and recall that γάνος, cognate with γαίω and γάνυμαι, contains in itself overtones of rejoicing). This is a subjective impression; more objectively, neither γαίω nor γηθέω comes with the best of credentials to the court of tragic diction. γαίω never occurs in tragedy and elsewhere is used only in the participle (in epic verse). Hesychius does have the entries γαίεσκον· ἔχαιρον and γαίειν· χαίρειν, γαυριᾶν, σεμνύνεσθαι, as well as the participial entries γαίων· γαυριῶν and γαίουσα· ὑπερφρονοῦσα. These entries cannot refer specifically to our passage, since, in Hesychius, such an entry would normally begin with the lemma γαίει. In fact, the entry γαίεσκον shows by its termination that it almost certainly does not come from tragedy at all: -σκε and -σκον are Epic and Ionic endings; in all extant tragedy only five examples of them are to be found (Kühner–Blass II, p. 81, Anmerk. 2). γηθέω is common enough in tragedy, but normally only in the perfect tense γέγηθα (with present meaning). According to LSJ, s.v. γηθέω, the "pf. is always used for pres. in Trag., unless γηθούσῃ φρενί be read in A. *Ch.* 772 [τάχιστα γαθούσῃ Turnebus *pro* τάχιστ' ἀγαθούσῃ], and impf. ἐπ-εγήθει in Id. *Pr.* 157 (lyr.) [ἐγεγήθει Elmsley]." There are two other possible occurrences in tragedy: *Prometheus* 760 γαθεῖν (Murray, anticipated by Schütz's γηθεῖν : μαθεῖν MSS) and Aeschylus frag. 474.831 (Mette), where Kamerbeek restored by conjecture ⟨γαθ⟩εῖ (⟨γηθ⟩εῖ Siegmann). If one must choose between γαίει and γαθεῖ, no hesitation is possible; γαθεῖ is clearly preferable. The scant evidence which survives is not fully conclusive, but it seems to me probable that Aeschylus on occasion did use the present γαθέω. (*Not* γηθέω, even in nonlyric passages. Compare below, sec. 78. This incidentally supports Elmsley's ἐγεγήθει against ἐπεγήθει of the MSS at *Prometheus* 157.) There can, of course, be no doubts about γάνος as a tragic word; it is certainly attested not only for Aeschylus but for Euripides. In a case such as this, it is legitimate to give full stress to the *ductus litterarum*. γᾶν εἰ is much more likely to be the product of a desperate attempt to make Greek out of an unintelligible γάνει than out of either γαίει or γαθεῖ. Granted that γαίει or γαθεῖ may have been just as unfamiliar as γάνει to a medieval scribe, who might then have tampered with them—but why would he have changed either of them to γᾶν εἰ, which is meaningless here? Rather, the man who wrote γᾶν εἰ was preserving the exact letters which he beheld in his exemplar; he did not understand the Greek, but the immediately following σπορητός suggested to him (unconsciously?) that a reference to γᾶν was apposite.

There is a further objection to Διὸς νότῳ, which has not been noticed. νότος does not mean "rain," though the defenders of the lection Διὸς νότῳ sometimes write as if it did; νότος is the *south wind*, which is, to be sure, a rain-bringing wind. In our passage, whether the thought be that a cornfield delights in the [rain-bringing] south wind or that a cornfield delights in the Zeus-given rain (Homer's Διὸς ὄμβρος), the sense is equally satisfactory. However, Διὸς νότος is not the same thing as either νότος or Διὸς ὄμβρος. In poetry νότος (or Νότος) often appears as a personal agent, as in *Iliad* 3.10 εὖτ᾽ ὄρεος κορυφῇσι Νότος κατέχευεν ὀμίχλην (see further *Odyssey* 3.295; 5.295, 331; 12.289, 325, 326, 427). Νότος, like the other winds, may take on the guise of a divinity in the poets; it is the personification—or rather deification—of the south wind. Hesiod so represents it in the *Theogony*; in fact, he tells us that Eos is the mother and *Astraeus* the *father* of Notos (and of Boreas and Zephyrus). See verses 378–380. Expressions such as Διὸς ὄμβρος or ὑέτιος νότος are fine Greek, no doubt; but somehow I have the feeling that Διὸς νότος is as un-Greek a conceit as Διὸς Βορέας would be.

Nor has it been observed that the Greeks by no means regarded the νότος as an *invariably* beneficent wind. Homer certainly represents it in quite the contrary light; the references have been given above. Hesiod, to be sure, in the *Theogony* (verse 871) describes the South Wind—in company with the North Wind and the West Wind—as θνητοῖς μέγ' ὄνειαρ. In the *Works and Days* (674–677), however, his advice is:

> μηδὲ μένειν οἶνόν τε νέον καὶ ὀπώρινον ὄμβρον
> καὶ χειμῶν' ἐπιόντα Νότοιό τε δεινὰς ἀήτας,
> ὅστ' ὤρινε θάλασσαν ὁμαρτήσας Διὸς ὄμβρῳ
> πολλῷ ὀπωρινῷ, χαλεπὸν δέ τε πόντον ἔθηκεν.

Sophocles described it as χειμέριος (*Antigone* 335), and Aristotle even states that it is καυματώδης (*Mete.* 364b23). The fact is that there is considerable documentation in Greek literature for the south wind as a destructive wind. Most telling of all for the Greek attitude toward the νότος is the evidence of the grammarians who tried to discover its etymology. Orion (p. 107.7 Sturz) states: Νότος παρὰ τὸ νόθους ποιεῖν τοὺς καρποὺς καὶ χείρους· οἷον ὀνοτοὺς ποιεῖν αὐτοὺς καὶ ἀφανίζειν; in the *Etymologicum Magnum* (p. 607.39 sq. Gaisford) the entry begins Νότος: ὁ ἄνεμος. Παρὰ τὸ ὀνῶ, τὸ βλάπτω, ὁ μέλλων ὀνόσω, ὄνοτος, καὶ νότος, ἀφαιρέσει τοῦ ō, οἱονεὶ ὁ βλαπτικὸς τῶν καρπῶν καὶ τῶν σωμάτων. This fanciful explanation is especially significant because the invented verb ὀνῶ (apparently inspired by ὄνομαι "blame"; the adjective ὀνοτός = ὀνοστός is a genuine form) is found elsewhere in the *EM*, where it is glossed not by τὸ βλάπτω but by τὸ ὠφελῶ (i.e. it was connected with ὀνίνημι). Had the grammarian wished, he could have derived νότος from ὀνῶ and still have given it a beneficent meaning!

Finally, in support of Διὸς νότῳ, Aeschylus frag. 44 (Nauck) has been compared; the context is a similar (i.e. "agricultural") one and in this fragment the expression ἐκ νοτίζοντος γάμου (γάνους Th. Gomperz!) occurs. This support is only apparent. νότος and νοτίζω, νοτίς, etc. come from the root *SNOT; νάω and Latin *natare* are cognate. The fundamental meaning of the root is something like "flow," "drip," "be moist or wet." νότος originally got its name because it was a *rainy* wind, not a *south* wind. As early as Homer, however, its primary significance had become "*south* wind." By contrast, most of the Greek words cognate with it (νοτερός, νοτέω, νοτίζω, νοτία, νοτίς) never have the connotation of "south," only of "wetness." This may be seen from such expressions as νοτερῷ βλεφάρῳ (Euripides), μύροισι νοτεῖ (Callimachus), νοτέων ἱδρώς (Nicander), νοτία φυσική (= "natural moisture of the body" Paulus Aegineta), νενοτισμένα οἴνῳ εἴρια ("Hippocrates"), νενοτισμένα δάκρυα (Meleager), ποντία νοτίς (Euripides); even νότιος, the regular adjective for "southern," often shows clearly its original meaning "wet," "moist": νότιος ἱδρώς (Homer), νοτίοις παγαῖς (Aeschylus), δίναις ἐν νοτίαις ἅλμας (Euripides). Such examples could be easily multiplied; nor is there any evidence that the ancients ever mistakenly derived νοτίζω, νοτίς, etc. from νότος. On the contrary, Aulus Gellius explicitly states (2.22.14): *is Latine auster, Graece* νότος *nominatur quoniam est nebulosus atque umectus*; νοτίς *enim Graece umor nominatur*, and the *Etymologicum Magnum*, *loc. cit.*, goes on to give an alternate derivation of νότος: Ἡ ἀπὸ τοῦ νοτεῖν καὶ τῆς νοτίδος· αὕτη δὲ ἡ Νοτὶς ... σημαίνει ... τὴν ὑγρασίαν. Aeschylus' use of νοτίζω elsewhere is inconclusive for our passage: νότος is not νοτίς, wind is not water.

§59

One of the chief culprits in distorting these verses of Aeschylus in the MSS was *false division*; it is a common cause of confusion. *Odyssey* 16.465–467:

οὐκ ἔμελέν μοι ταῦτα μεταλλῆσαι καὶ ἐρέσθαι

ἄστυ καταβλώσκοντα· τάχιστά με θυμὸς ἀνώγει
ἀγγελίην εἰπόντα πάλιν δεῦρ᾽ ἀπονέεσθαι.

Though most editors print καταβλώσκοντα here, the variant κάτα βλώσκοντα is to be preferred. The speaker, Eumaeus, is answering Telemachus' question τί δὴ κλέος ἔστ᾽ ἀνὰ ἄστυ; "It was not my concern," he replies, "*to go all around the town* and inquire about these matters." καταβλώσκω would mean simply "go down to"; the verb is found nowhere else in Homer. For the expression ἄστυ κάτα βλώσκοντα there are several parallels:

... κέλεαι κατὰ ἄστυ ἀλήμεναι αὖτις ἰόντας

(Il. 18.286)

... κατὰ πτόλιν οἴχετο πάντῃ

(Od. 2.383)

τὸν δ᾽   ... οὐκ ἐνόησαν
ἐρχόμενον κατὰ ἄστυ

(Od. 7.39–40)

        ... ἀλαλήμενος αἰεὶ
ἄστυ κάτ᾽

(Od. 17.245–246)

        ... κατὰ ἄστυ
πτωχεύεσκ᾽ ...

(Od. 18.1–2)

        ... ἐάσομεν οὐδὲ θύγατρας
οὐδ᾽ ἄλοχον κεδνὴν Ἰθάκης κατὰ ἄστυ πολεύειν.

(Od. 22.222–223)

Eustathius apparently read the simple verb here, for he comments τὸ δὲ βλώσκοντα δύναται γραφῆναι καὶ βλώσκοντι κατὰ πτῶσιν δοτικὴν ... (p. 1809.17–18). A similar case is *Iliad* 4.229–230:

τῷ μάλα πόλλ᾽ ἐπέτελλε παρισχέμεν, ὁππότε κέν μιν
γυῖα λάβῃ κάματος, πολέας διὰ κοιρανέοντα.

§59. False Division

Some MSS have a *varia lectio* διακοιρανέοντα. Eustathius (p. 465.44) annotates στρατηγικὸν μόχθον ἐν πολέμῳ δηλοῖ τὸ ὁππότε ⟨κέν⟩ μιν γυῖα λάβοι κάματος πολέας κατακοιρανέοντα. Whether κατακοιρανέοντα is a mere *lapsus memoriae* or a genuine variant, it shows that Eustathius (or his source) read a compound verb here. As in the *Odyssey* passage, it is better to govern the accusative by the preposition and print *divisim* πολέας διὰ κοιρανέοντα. The *simplex* κοιρανέω is common in Homer, διακοιρανέω would be a ἅπαξ λεγόμενον. That the ambiguity was recognized and discussed in antiquity is shown by the entry in Hesychius διακοιρανέοντα· βασιλικῶς ἐπερχόμενον, ἢ ὡς κοίρανον διαπορευόμενον, διέποντα. The accusative singular termination of the entry leaves no reasonable doubt that the reference is to the present passage. The scholiast at *Iliad* 5.332 (πόλεμον κάτα κοιρανέουσιν) is quite explicit about such ambiguities: ὁ Ἀσκαλωνίτης ἀναστρέφει, ἵνα γένηται κατὰ πόλεμον. δύναται δὲ ἔμφασις γενέσθαι, εἰ συνάπτοιτο τῷ κοιρανέουσιν, ὡς ἀνακοιρανέοντα [sc. *Il.* 5.824 μάχην ἀνὰ κοιρανέοντα]· καὶ ἔστιν ὅμοιον τὸ Ἰθάκην κατακοιρανέουσιν [*Od.* 1.247, *alibi*]. Hesychius has still another entry: κατακοιρανέοντα· κατακοσμοῦντα. The editor of Hesychius, Kurt Latte, doubtfully referred this as a variant reading to *Iliad* 5.824 μάχην ἀνὰ κοιρανέοντα. This reference is made unlikely by Hesychius' explanation κατακοσμοῦντα; κοσμεῖν is applied not to *battles* but to *people* in Homer (so often in a military sense). (It must be acknowledged, though, that expressions such as ἀρτύνθη δὲ μάχη, *Il.* 11.216, show that this argument cannot be pressed too much.) If the entry refers to any extant passage, it is probably to *Iliad* 4.230 πολέας διὰ κοιρανέοντα, where Eustathius (quoted above) also seems to preserve traces of a variant κατακοιρανέοντα.

It is well known that a number of Homeric words are actually the result of unconscious false division; familiar examples are (ν)ήδυμος and (ὁ)κρυόεις. The phenomenon is not restricted to Homer. Plutarch, *Moralia* p. 1109A, preserves a fragment of Democritus (156 Diels–Kranz): . . . διορίζεται [sc. Δημόκριτος] μὴ μᾶλλον τὸ δὲν ἢ τὸ μηδὲν εἶναι, δὲν μὲν ὀνομάζων τὸ σῶμα, μηδὲν δὲ τὸ κενόν, ὡς καὶ τούτου φύσιν τινὰ καὶ ὑπόστασιν ἰδίαν ἔχοντος. Compare the fragment of

91

Alcaeus (320 Lobel–Page), preserved in the grammatical tradition: καί κ' οὐδὲν ἐκ δενὸς γένοιτο. In these instances the division is conscious, but made in the genuine belief that οὐδέν was a compound of οὐ and δέν. Compare Theodotion's version of Genesis 1.2: ἡ δὲ γῆ ἦν θὲν καὶ οὐθέν. By the Hellenistic period, whimsey, pure and simple, was coining new words. When Hermesianax, in the third book of his *Leontion*, writes that Hesiod Ἑοίην μνώμενος Ἀσκραϊκήν | πόλλ' ἔπαθεν (frag. 7.24–25 Powell), the young lady in question, Ἑοίη, is nothing but the personification of the familiar Hesiodic tag ἢ οἵη, which gave its name to the *Ehoiai* (ἢ οἷαι) or *Catalogue of Women*. In two "technopaegnia," the *Altar* of Dosiadas (verse 1) and the *Syrinx* of Theocritus (? verse 14), the word στήτα is used for γυνή. This is a coinage based on deliberate false division of the familiar words at the opening of the *Iliad* διαστήτην ἐρίσαντε: the dual form διαστήτην was divided to make a prepositional phrase διὰ στήτην, "on account of a woman." From this was extrapolated στήτη, which, in Doric dress, becomes στήτα. No one, I think, will see in this an unintentional confusion. I cite these examples of deliberate false divisions to point out that they were most likely to be perpetrated at a time when writing conditions were such as to make accidental false division a common error: In the history of Greek writing, the so-called *scriptio continua* was the normal practice from the very beginning up to the end of the uncial period in Byzantine times.

§60. Apollonius Rhodius *Argonautica* 2. 1125-1127

πόντῳ γὰρ τρηχεῖαι ἐπιβρίσασαι ἄελλαι
νηὸς ἀεικελίης διὰ δούρατα πάντ' ἐκέδασσαν
ᾗ ἔνι †τειρόμενοι ἄμ' ἐπὶ† χρέος ἐμβεβαῶτες.

What Apollonius wrote in verse 1127 was

ᾗ ἔνι πείρομεν οἶδμα κατὰ χρέος ἐμβεβαῶτες.

92

πείρομεν οἶδμα was conjectured independently by J. H. Voss and H. Koechly; the phrase is supported by Apollonius' usage elsewhere: οἶδμα περῆσαι (3.388), ᾗ νηὶ διὲξ ἁλὸς οἶδμα περήσας (4.457), πεῖρον ἁλὸς μέγα λαῖτμα (4.980). Nevertheless, the emendation failed to win universal acceptance; in 1932 it was confirmed by the publication of a Berlin papyrus fragment containing several scholia to Apollonius (edited by A. Wifstrand in *Eranos* 30 [1932] 1–6). Koechly further conjectured κατὰ χρέος, which is supported by 4.530 ... Αἰσονίδη περόωντι κατὰ χρέος; see also 1.660, 3.189, 4.889 (Platt in *JP* 34 [1915] 134–135). This usage of κατά is well illustrated by an epigram which has come down to us under Simonides' name (frag. 138 Diehl):

> Κρὴς γενεὰν Βρόταχος Γορτύνιος ἐνθάδε κεῖμαι
> οὐ κατὰ τοῦτ' ἐλθών, ἀλλὰ κατ' ἐμπορίαν.

Metrically οἶδμα ἐπὶ χρέος is very doubtful (hiatus after οἶδμα which terminates in an elidable vowel?); see Fränkel's monograph, cited below.

The corruption had two stages: (1) the uncial letters ΠΕΙΡΟΜΕ-ΝΟΙΔΜΑ were misread as ΤΕΙΡΟΜΕΝΟΙΑΜΑ and falsely divided; (2) the resultant τειρόμενοι ἄμα κατὰ would not scan, so that ἄμα κατὰ was consciously altered to ἄμ' ἐπὶ to heal the meter. For a full and lucid discussion of the history of this verse, the reader should consult H. Fränkel, *Einleitung zur kritischen Ausgabe der Argonautika des Apollonius* (Göttingen 1964) 23–25; my indebtedness to Professor Fränkel's monograph for my treatment of this passage is hereby acknowledged with pleasure and gratitude.

§61. *Homeric Hymn to Demeter* 6–8

ἄνθεά τ' αἰνυμένην ῥόδα καὶ κρόκον ἠδ' ἴα καλὰ
λειμῶν' ἄμ μαλακὸν καὶ ἀγαλλίδας ἠδ' ὑάκινθον
ναρκισσόν θ' ...

λειμῶν' ἄμ Hermann (ἂν Ruhnken) : λειμῶνα

Sense, grammar, and meter all demand a preposition here; the correction of λειμῶνα μαλακὸν to λειμῶν' ἀ⟨μ⟩ μαλακὸν is self-evident. Haplography (and dittography) of identical letters is common; such deviations in the MSS, slight though they seem, often materially affect the meaning of a passage, as in the following example.

§62. Gregorius Nyssenus *Epistolae* 1.5 (p. 4.11-16 Pasquali²)

   . . . καὶ τέλος, τὴν μνήμην τοῦ μακαριωτάτου Πέτρου παρὰ Σεβαστηνοῖς πρώτως ἀγομένην ἐπιτελέσας, καὶ τὰς συνήθως παρ' αὐτῶν ἐπιτελουμένας τῶν ἁγίων ⟨μ'⟩ μαρτύρων μνήμας κατὰ τὸν αὐτὸν χρόνον συνδιαγαγὼν ἐκείνοις, ἐπὶ τὴν ἐμαυτοῦ πάλιν ἐκκλησίαν ὑπέστρεφον.

Jaeger's ingenious addition of μ' (the normal abbreviation for τεττα-ράκοντα) before μαρτύρων makes the general reference to martyrs quite specific: Gregory is alluding to the forty martyrs of Sebaste, whose feast day now falls on the ninth of March. (Pasquali in his edition gives the fourth of March as the date, but this is an error. See the entry for March 9 in the *Synaxarion Ecclesiae Constantinopolitanae*, printed in the *Propylaeum ad Acta Sanctorum Novembris* [Brussels 1902], pp. 521–524.) Three sermons by Gregory on the forty martyrs of Sebaste are still extant (Migne, *PG* 46.749–788).

Some notion of the ease and frequency of haplographies may be suggested by the following brief sentence from the *Epitome* of the *Bibliotheca* of "Apollodorus" (6.30): . . . ἐλθὼν δὲ εἰς Σπάρτην ⟨τὴν⟩ ἰδίαν ἐκτήσατο βασιλείαν. The reference is to Menelaus' return to Sparta after the Trojan War. Frazer translates "And having come to Sparta he regained his own kingdom," which is the meaning wanted. Of the two witnesses for the *Epitome*, E (= codex Vaticanus 950) preserves τὴν after Σπάρτην; it is omitted in the other witness S (= codex Sabbaiticus-Hierosolymitanus 366). Professor John Shea of Catholic

University pointed out to me that the sense demands that we read ⟨ἀν⟩εκτήσατο, "re-gained"; ἀν- dropped out after the termination -αν. Thus in S the single word ἰδίαν is both preceded and followed by a haplography.

§63. Gregorius Nyssenus *Epistolae* 2.12 (p. 17.6-10 Pasquali[2])

καὶ ἐπειδὴ ὅμορός ἐστιν ἡ Ἀραβία τοῖς κατὰ Ἱεροσόλυμα τό-
ποις, †ὑποσχόμενος καὶ συσκεψάμενος† τοῖς προεστῶσι τῶν ἐν
Ἱεροσολύμοις ἁγίων ἐκκλησιῶν διὰ τὸ εἶναι αὐτῶν ἐν ταραχῇ
τὰ πράγματα καὶ χρῄζειν τοῦ μεσιτεύοντος.

Jaeger's ὑπεσχόμην ὡς καὶ συσκεψόμενος restores the desired main verb; the false division was easy and understandable (recall that ως and ος were identical in sound).

§64. Plutarch *Moralia* 367D (*De Iside et Osiride* 41)

... Τυφῶνα μὲν οἴονται τὸν ἡλιακὸν κόσμον, Ὄσιριν δὲ τὸν
σεληνιακὸν λέγεσθαι. τὴν μὲν γὰρ σελήνην γόνιμον τὸ φῶς καὶ
ὑγροποιὸν ἔχουσαν εὐμενῆ καὶ γοναῖς ζῴων καὶ φυτῶν εἶναι
βλαστήσεσι· τὸν δ' ἥλιον ἀκράτῳ πυρὶ καὶ σκληρῷ καταθάλπειν
τε καὶ καταυαίνειν τὰ φυόμενα καὶ τεθηλότα κτλ.

καὶ σκληρῷ καταθάλπειν Madvig : κεκληρωκότα θάλπειν MSS

Madvig's solution (partially anticipated by Wyttenbach, who wrote καὶ σκληροτάτῳ) is quite convincing; the intensifying compound καταυαίνειν commends καταθάλπειν and the word order ἀκράτῳ πυρὶ καὶ σκληρῷ is supported by the parallel order above γόνιμον τὸ φῶς καὶ ὑγροποιὸν (a phrase which would not argue for reading ἀκράτῳ ⟨τῷ⟩ πυρὶ here: γόνιμον . . . καὶ ὑγροποιὸν are predicates, as regularly in Greek with ἔχειν; contrast 368C below . . . ὅταν φῶς ἐρείσῃ γόνιμον ἀπὸ τῆς σελήνης . . .). The corruption is extremely easy, and could have come about in several ways (και and κε were pronounced identically, καί is very frequently abbreviated, uncial sigma and epsilon are often confused . . .).

§65. Pseudo-Xenophon *Athenaion Politeia* 2.12

πρὸς δὲ τούτοις [sc. οἱ Ἀθηναῖοι] ἄλλοσε ἄγειν οὐκ ἐάσουσιν †οἵτινες ἀντίπαλοι ἡμῖν εἰσιν ἢ οὐ χρήσονται τῇ θαλάττῃ.

post ἐάσουσιν lac. stat. Schmidt : ἐάσουσι ⟨πρὸς τούτους⟩ Hofmann

In this sentence the "Old Oligarch" is saying that the Athenians will not permit exportation (of shipbuilding materials) to any place where they have enemies; those who attempt such exportation shall be barred from the use of the sea. (ἢ here means "or else"; compare Eur. *Phoen.* 593, *HF* 1055, *Or.* 537, 1612; And. 1.33; Pl. *Phaedr.* 237C; Herod. 5.74; Plut. *Sol.* 21.) Hofmann's ⟨πρὸς τούτους⟩ restores the sense, but one wonders how probable it is that a Greek would write πρὸς δὲ τούτοις . . . πρὸς τούτους in such proximity; furthermore, the corruption would not be readily explicable. The solution is closer to hand: read οἷ τινες for οἵτινες; the Attic idiom is ἄλλοσε οἷ. That scribes would misunderstand ΟΙΤΙΝΕC here was inevitable. (I have discussed this passage in *CP* 58 [1963] 38.)

§66. Epicurus frag. 163 Usener (= frag. 33 Bailey)

παιδείαν δὲ πᾶσαν, μακάριε, φεῦγε τἀκάτιον ἀράμενος.

This fragment has been preserved by Diogenes Laertius 10.6, where the MSS are all variously corrupt: φευγετε κατιδιαραμεν B : φεύγε τε κατι δι ἔραμεν P: φεύγετε Fᵃᶜ: φεύγετε καταδιέρα Fᵖᶜ. φεῦγε τἀκάτιον ἀράμενος is Gassendi's correction; it is confirmed by a passage in Plutarch *De Audiendis Poetis* 15D: πότερον οὖν τῶν νέων ὥσπερ τῶν Ἰθακησίων σκληρῷ τινι τὰ ὦτα καὶ ἀτέγκτῳ κηρῷ καταπλάσσοντες ἀναγκάζωμεν αὐτοὺς τὸ Ἐπικούρειον ἀκάτιον ἀραμένους ποιητικὴν φεύγειν καὶ παρεξελαύνειν, ἢ μᾶλλον κτλ. (Compare also Quintilian *Inst.* 12.2.24: *nam in primis nos Epicurus a se ipse dimittit, qui fugere omnem disciplinam navigatione quam velocissima iubet.*) The erroneous plural ΦΕΥΓΕΤΕ, the product of a false division, was the start of the corruption; the resultant nonsense ΚΑΤΙΟΝΑΡΑΜΕΝΟC was then especially liable to further corruption. In particular, ΝΑ was then misread as ΔΙΑ, an easy confusion in uncials.

§67. Epicurus *Κύριαι Δόξαι* 11 (= Diogenes Laertius 10.142)

Εἰ μηθὲν ἡμᾶς αἱ τῶν μετεώρων ὑποψίαι ἠνώχλουν καὶ αἱ περὶ θανάτου, μή ποτε πρὸς ἡμᾶς ᾖ τι, ἔτι τε τὸ μὴ κατανοεῖν τοὺς ὅρους τῶν ἀλγηδόνων καὶ τῶν ἐπιθυμιῶν, οὐκ ἂν προσεδεόμεθα φυσιολογίας.

τε τὸ μὴ κατανοεῖν Lachelier : τετόλμηκα νοεῖν

Bailey translates "If we were not troubled by our suspicions of the phenomena of the sky and about death, fearing that it concerns us, and also by our failure to grasp the limits of pains and desires, we should have no need of natural science." Lachelier's conjecture has considerable probability. The corruption could have easily occurred; it is wrong to demand or expect always an exact letter-for-letter correspondence between a corrupt MS lection and the restored text. Nor is it realistic to look for certitude where it is not forthcoming, as in the following passage.

§68. Epicurus Κύριαι Δόξαι 37 (= Diogenes Laertius 10.152)

... κἂν μεταπίπτῃ τὸ κατὰ τὸ δίκαιον συμφέρον, χρόνον δέ τινα εἰς τὴν πρόληψιν ἐναρμόττῃ, οὐδὲν ἧττον ἐκεῖνον τὸν χρόνον ἦν δίκαιον τοῖς μὴ φωναῖς κεναῖς ἑαυτοὺς συνταράττουσιν ἀλλὰ †πλεῖστα† πράγματα βλέπουσιν.

ἀλλ᾽ [απλ] εἰς τὰ Usener : ἀλλ᾽ ἀπλ<ῶς> εἰς τὰ Kochalsky

It is certain that the transmitted text is not sound; the conjectures of both Usener and Kochalsky are possible. (For the expression Gomperz compared Philodemus, *Volumina Rhetorica* 1.286 Sudhaus, εἰς [πρ]άγματα βλέποντος.) Editors are divided. Bailey and von der Muehll print ἀλλ᾽ εἰς τὰ (Bailey, however, acknowledges that Kochalsky's conjecture may be right and von der Muehll seems not to know of it); R. D. Hicks and H. S. Long in their editions of Diogenes Laertius print ἀλλ᾽ ἀπλῶς εἰς τὰ, which seems more probable to me. (Paleographically, the haplography of ως before εις with the resultant false division is much easier than to assume, as Bailey does, that ἀ πλ is a dittography of ἀλλ᾽.)

§69. Aristotle *Metaphysica* 1007b11–17

... οὐδὲ δὴ τῷ λευκῷ ἕτερόν τι ἔσται συμβεβηκός, οἷον τὸ μουσικόν· οὐθέν τε γὰρ μᾶλλον τοῦτο ἐκείνῳ ἢ ἐκεῖνο τούτῳ συμβέβηκεν, καὶ ἅμα διώρισται ὅτι τὰ μὲν οὕτω συμβέβηκε τὰ δ᾽ ὡς τὸ μουσικὸν Σωκράτει· ὅσα δ᾽ οὕτως, οὐ συμβεβηκότι συμβέβηκε τὸ συμβεβηκός, ἀλλ᾽ ὅσα ἐκείνως, ὥστ᾽ οὐ πάντα κατὰ συμβεβηκὸς λεχθήσεται. ἔσται ἄρα τι καὶ <οὔτ>ως οὐσίαν σημαῖνον.

<οὔτ>ως Jaeger : ὡς codd. : ὧς Ross

For καὶ ὡς οὐσίαν of the MSS Ross conjectured καὶ ὧς οὐσίαν. In his commentary he writes: "In the vulgate reading καὶ ὡς οὐσίαν σημαῖ-

νον, ὡς is superfluous. I have therefore read *καὶ ὡς*, 'even so'. Cf. *De Caelo* 302b24, *De Sensu* 444b5, and *D.G.C.* 329b3, where Prof. Joachim has made the same correction." Joachim at *De Gen. et Corr.* 329b3-4 comments: "The use of *ὡς* for *οὕτως* is rare in Aristotle: but cf. *de Caelo* 302b24." Whether Aristotle wrote *καὶ οὕτως* or *καὶ ὡς* in the *Metaphysics* passage is a matter of small import, for the sense is the same with either reading. (Nor do I think that we can decide *with certainty* between *καὶ οὕτως* and *καὶ ὡς*.) There is, however, a fundamental principle of textual criticism involved here; Jaeger in the *apparatus* to his edition of the *Metaphysics* puts the case quite succinctly: "*οὕτως* correxi: *ὡς* codd.: *ὡς* Ross quae facilior esset emendatio, sed minus id est Aristotelicum." In the fairly ample Aristotelian corpus *ὡς* for *οὕτως* is barely attested; that is to say, it is not at all typical of Aristotle's *style*. Jaeger showed himself a critic of sound method in attaching more importance to his author's style than to a seductive *ductus litterarum*—and this principle is just as true even if Aristotle in fact happened to have written *καὶ ὡς* here! The case, as I have indicated, does not admit of certainty. (It should perhaps be added that ⟨οὕτ⟩*ως*, while admittedly not so easy a correction paleographically as *ὡς*, is by no means an improbable one. *Exempli gratia*, *οὕτ* could have been accidentally omitted under the influence of the following *οὐσίαν*; I do not have a technical name for this sort of psychological anticipatory omission, but I do know that such things happen in transcription. An alternate explanation is to regard *καὶ ὡς* as an unconscious substitution made by a copyist who himself in everyday speech used *καὶ ὡς* rather than its synonym *καὶ οὕτως*.)

§70. Gorgias *Palamedes* 22 (Diels-Kranz, *Vorsokr.*[10] 2.299.22-24)

βούλομαι δὲ μετὰ ταῦτα πρὸς τὸν κατήγορον διαλεχθῆναι. τίνι ποτὲ πιστεύσας τοιοῦτος ὢν τοιούτου κατηγορεῖς; ἄξιον γὰρ καταμαθεῖν, οἷος ὢν οἷα λέγεις ὡς ἀνάξιος ἀναξίῳ.

οἷα λέγεις ὡς Blass : οἶδάς γε ἴσως

The transmitted words οἶδάς γε ἴσως are clearly corrupt. Even if sense could be forced from them, the form οἶδας is suspicious; the usual form οἶσθα occurs in this very chapter, and below in chapter 24 both οἶσθα and σύνοισθα occur. Blass's οἷα λέγεις ὡς is quite ingenious; if we put the letters into uncial *scriptura continua*, as Blass did, the error becomes immediately understandable: ΟΙΑΛΕΓΕΙϹΩϹ→ΟΙΔΑϹ-ΓΕΙϹΩϹ. Nevertheless, despite the neatness of the exact paleographical correspondence, I am not fully convinced of this solution. οἷα destroys the studied balance of the passage (τοιοῦτος ὢν τοιούτου κατηγορεῖς ... ἀνάξιος ἀναξίῳ); read οἷος ὢν οἵῳ λέγεις ὡς ἀνάξιος ἀναξίῳ. It was easy enough for a copyist who had misdivided at -ΓΕ ΙϹΩϹ to misread ΟΙΩΛΕ as a verb ΟΙΔΑϹ; it should be noted that in the very next line forms of οἶδα occur three times. Blass is to be congratulated for first seeing the way to resolve this *crux*; the requirements of sense and style suggest that he did not go quite far enough.

Whether one prefers οἷα or οἵῳ, there is little doubt that Gorgias has here combined two case-forms of οἷος for stylistic effect. This provides strong support, hitherto unnoticed, for a commonly accepted correction in Plato's *Symposium* (195A):

εἷς δὲ τρόπος ὀρθὸς παντὸς ἐπαίνου περὶ παντός, λόγῳ διελθεῖν οἷος <οἵ>ων αἴτιος ὢν τυγχάνει περὶ οὗ ἂν ὁ λόγος ᾖ.

The MSS give οἷος ὢν (or ὧν or both); codex T, according to Burnet, has οἷος οἵων *ex emendatione*, and this is what most editors print, though a few (for example Rettig and Robin) prefer οἷος ὢν. For the collocation οἷος οἵων Schmelzer and Harder, in their edition of the *Symposium*, compare *Phaedrus* 271B and Sophocles *Trachiniae* 1045 (in both of which passages two cases of οἷος are coupled). What makes the parallel in Gorgias' *Palamedes* especially relevant here is the fact that this sentence comes from Agathon's speech—and in that speech Plato is deliberately imitating and parodying Gorgias' style. Compare Socrates' jest at the conclusion of the speech about the Γοργίου κεφαλή (198C).

§71

The reader is well advised to attend to the most minor details of style; his efforts will result in a surer and clearer command of a writer's chief stylistic distinctions. In Isocrates *Encomium Helenae* 21 editors now print . . . τοῦτον δὲ μόνον οὐδ' ἑνὸς ἐνδεᾶ γενόμενον . . ., where οὐδ' ἑνὸς is Benseler's conjecture for οὐδενὸς of the MSS (οὐθ' ἑνὸς Λ). If we are to believe LSJ s.v. οὐδείς B, "the more emphatic and literal sense, *not even one*, i.e. *none whatever*, belongs to the full form, οὐδὲ εἷς, οὐδὲ μία, οὐδὲ ἕν, which is never elided, even in Com. . . ., but freq. has a Particle inserted between." The same mistake has been made by Burnet at Plato *Cratylus* 400C9, where he writes οὐδ' ἕν for οὐδὲν (with the variant οὐδὲ) of the MSS. At Plato *Symposium* 213D2 modern editors generally print οὐδ' ἑνί, where the best MSS have in fact οὐδενί. Such insignificant stylistic features can sometimes be of real importance. See *Hermes* 92 (1964) 507–508, where I believe that I have demonstrated, beyond reasonable doubt, the existence in Iamblichus of a genuine fragment from Aristotle's lost dialogue *Protrepticus*. (The reality of such Aristotelian remains in Iamblichus has been a matter of some debate in recent years.) Among other proofs, I point out that the phrase in Iamblichus καταλείπεται τὸ διανοεῖσθαι καὶ θεωρεῖν involves a construction so uncommon that it is unattested in the lexica: λείπεται and καταλείπεται regularly take the *simple* infinitive, not the *articular* infinitive. Aristotle, however, on occasion affects the articular construction; I cite several examples. Here is a case where the presence of a single τό was the decisive factor. Compare the comment of D. A. Russell in his edition of "Longinus" *On The Sublime*, p. xxv n. 1: "One small point: L [i.e. pseudo-Longinus] almost makes a mannerism of πάντες ἑξῆς and the like (4.4, 9.14, 33.5, 34.3): Longinus (fr. VII Toup) has πάντες ἐφεξῆς. This is the sort of detail which makes good evidence for a difference of author."

§72. Arrian *Anabasis* 1.27.7

ταῦτα δὴ ἰδὼν ᾿Αλέξανδρος στρατοπεδεύεσθαι αὐτοῦ, ὅπως
εἶχον, ἐκέλευε τοὺς Μακεδόνας, γνοὺς ὅτι οὐ μενοῦσι πανδημεὶ
οἱ Τελμισσεῖς αὐλιζομένους σφᾶς ἰδόντες, ἀλλ᾿ ἀποχωρήσουσιν
ἐς τὴν πόλιν πλησίον οὖσαν οἱ πολλοὶ αὐτῶν, ὅσον φυλακὴν κατα-
λιπόντες ἐπὶ τοῖς ὄρεσι. καὶ ξυνέβη ὅπως εἴκαζεν.

The imperfect εἴκαζεν is the reading of the MSS and is retained by the
Teubner editor Roos and the Loeb editor Robson (who defends it with
the too general statement ". . . here as elsewhere Arrian does not ob-
serve Attic precision"). Sintenis conjectured εἴκασεν and Boehner (*De
Arriani dicendi genere*, in *Acta Seminarii Philol. Erlang.* 4, p. 34) cited as
parallels for the aorist the following passages from the *Anabasis*:

(1.1.9) καὶ οὕτω ξυνέβη ὅπως παρήνεσέ τε ᾿Αλέξανδρος καὶ
εἴκασεν.

(2.10.3) καὶ ξυνέβη ὅπως εἴκασεν ᾿Αλέξανδρος.

(4.2.5) καὶ ξυνέβη τε οὕτως ὅπως εἴκασε . . .

(5.23.4) . . . καὶ ἅμα εἰκάσας ὅτι φοβεροὶ γενόμενοι οἱ ᾿Ινδοὶ
. . . ἀπολείψουσι τῆς νυκτὸς τὴν πόλιν. καὶ ξυνέβη οὕτως ὅπως
εἴκασεν.

The tense that one would naturally expect in such expressions is the
aorist, and these parallels leave no doubt what Arrian's actual practice
was. In 1.27.7 εἴκαζεν is not impossible; it is simply improbable in the
extreme. Sintenis' εἴκασεν should be adopted without hesitation; the
scribal confusion εἴκασεν/εἴκαζεν is of the easiest sort. In 5.23.7

. . . ὁ δὲ Πτολεμαῖον τὸν Λάγου ἐπιτάττει ἐνταῦθα, τῶν τε
ὑπασπιστῶν αὐτῷ δοὺς χιλιαρχίας τρεῖς καὶ τοὺς ᾿Αγριᾶνας
ξύμπαντας καὶ μίαν τάξιν τῶν τοξοτῶν, ἀποδείξας τὸ χωρίον,
ἧπερ μάλιστα εἴκαζε βιάσεσθαι τοὺς βαρβάρους κτλ.

Krüger wished to read ἧπερ μάλιστα εἴκασε; but in this passage the imperfect has its normal force and there is no reason to tamper with it. The passages listed above are not parallel (as Krüger seemed to think). Arrian *could* have written εἴκασε here; there is no evidence to show that he did. If parallels for the imperfect are demanded (they are unnecessary), I have two to offer:

(6.12.2) . . . τῶν μὲν [sc. ἐθνῶν] οὔπω προσκεχωρηκότων, ἃ δὴ ὑπὲρ τῆς ἐλευθερίας εἴκαζον ἀγωνιεῖσθαι καρτερῶς . . .

(6.12.3) . . . οὐδὲ ταῦτα τοῖς πολλοῖς ὑπὸ τοῦ ἄγαν δέους πιστὰ ἐφαίνετο, ἀλλὰ πλάττεσθαι γὰρ πρὸς τῶν ἀμφ᾽ αὐτὸν σωματο-φυλάκων τε καὶ στρατηγῶν εἰκάζετο.

In the second passage notice that εἰκάζετο is passive; the aorist would have been εἰκάσθη, and thus the possibility of an accidental confusion of σ and ζ is excluded. To return to the original passage, 1.27.7: Roos and Robson, in refusing to give up εἴκαζε of the MSS for Sintenis' εἴκασε, reveal themselves to be, by implication at least, practitioners of a theory of textual criticism, the fundamental principle of which is clearly stated by Marchant on the first page of the *Praefatio* to his Oxford edition of Xenophon: *Imprimis autem id mihi agendum arbitratus sum ut quae in libris manuscriptis tradita erant ea, si ullo modo tolerari possent, in textu retinerem potius quam coniecturam acciperem veri quidem simillimam, sed non fatalem, ut ita dicam, et necessariam.* Such an approach to the texts is one even today favored by not a few scholars. Of this "method" let it suffice to say that it is false and that no eminent critic since the days of Joseph Justus Scaliger and Richard Bentley has espoused it.

§73

There are of course literally thousands of passages where the readings of the MSS have been unnecessarily condemned and tampered with by scholars. R. J. White (*Dr. Bentley*, p. 221) aptly refers to the "occupational disease of the 'emendator'—the final inability to leave well alone." Bentley and Wilamowitz have provided us with the most brilliant examples of this particular aberration, but Dr. Verrall certainly deserves honorable mention. The psychology underlying this tendency has been succinctly described by Aristotle in one of his *obiter dicta*: πάντες ἀγαπῶσι μᾶλλον τὰ αὐτῶν ἔργα, ὥσπερ οἱ γονεῖς καὶ οἱ ποιηταί. Take Marcus Aurelius *Meditations* 5.33.6: . . . τί ἀρκεῖ; τί δ' ἄλλο ἢ θεοὺς μὲν σέβειν καὶ εὐφημεῖν, ἀνθρώπους δὲ εὖ ποιεῖν καὶ ἀνέχεσθαι αὐτῶν καὶ ἀπέχεσθαι. Trannoy, the Budé editor, comments "καὶ ἀπέχεσθαι secludam, nisi scribas: κ. μὴ ἀπέχθεσθαι." *At nil mutandum*; the MSS are quite sound. Marcus Aurelius was a *Stoic* philosopher; Aulus Gellius (17.19.6), on the authority of Favorinus, tells us that that other great Stoic of the second century, Epictetus, "verba haec duo dicebat: ἀνέχου et ἀπέχου." The phrase was obviously a Stoic byword; I have seen it echoed in the extant remains of Epictetus: βλέπε, πῶς ἐσθίω, πῶς πίνω, πῶς καθεύδω, πῶς ἀνέχομαι, πῶς ἀπέχομαι κτλ. (4.8.20; compare 2.22.20).

In Pseudo–Xenophon *Ath. Pol.* 1.6 almost every editor prints the following:

> εἴποι δ' ἄν τις ὡς ἐχρῆν αὐτοὺς μὴ ἐᾶν λέγειν πάντας ἐξ ἴσης
> μηδὲ βουλεύειν, ἀλλὰ τοὺς δεξιωτάτους καὶ ἄνδρας ἀρίστους . . .
>
> ἐξ ἴσης Bergk : ἑξῆς MSS

Frisch, for example, accepting ἐξ ἴσης, which he renders "on an equal footing," comments "The reading of the MSS is ἑξῆς, which means 'in a row,' but the context seems to require ἐξ ἴσης as proposed by Bergk." The only objection to Bergk's conjecture is that it is quite unnecessary. ἑξῆς does mean "in a row," "in strict sequence," "in arithmetical succession"; however, scholars have apparently failed to notice that ἑξῆς (and ἐφεξῆς) is often idiomatically combined with forms of πᾶς in a quite "unmathematical" sense. πάντες ἑξῆς means simply "everybody," "each and every one"; the Italian *tutti quanti* has a similar force. This idiom is as old as Homer (*Iliad* 6.240–241): ὁ δ' ἔπειτα θεοῖς εὔχεσθαι ἀνώγει / πάσας ἑξείης. A very clear example of it is Thucydides 7.29.4 . . . τοὺς ἀνθρώπους ἐφόνευον φειδόμενοι οὔτε πρεσβυτέρας οὔτε νεωτέρας ἡλικίας, ἀλλὰ πάντας ἑξῆς, ὅτῳ ἐντύχοιεν, καὶ παῖδας καὶ γυναῖκας κτείνοντες. Another instance is Euripides frag. 657.1–2 Nauck:

> ὅστις δὲ πάσας συντιθεὶς ψέγει λόγῳ
> γυναῖκας ἑξῆς, σκαιός ἐστι κοὐ σοφός.

It occurs in Plato *Symposium* 195E: ἐν γὰρ ἤθεσι καὶ ψυχαῖς θεῶν καὶ ἀνθρώπων τὴν οἴκησιν ἵδρυται [sc. ὁ "Ερως], καὶ οὐκ αὖ ἑξῆς ἐν πάσαις ταῖς ψυχαῖς, ἀλλ᾽ ᾗτινι ἂν σκληρὸν ἦθος ἐχούσῃ ἐντύχῃ, ἀπέρχεται, ᾗ δ᾽ ἂν μαλακόν, οἰκίζεται. Here, unfamiliarity with the idiom prompted a friend of mine to conjecture εἰκῇ for ἑξῆς. For ἅπαντες ἑξῆς in "Longinus," see D. A. Russell's edition, p. xxv n. 1 (quoted above, sec. 71 *ad fin.*). Professor Christopher Jones kindly called my attention to the certain instance of the idiom in Demosthenes 9.69: ... χρὴ καὶ ναύτην καὶ κυβερνήτην καὶ πάντ᾽ ἄνδρ᾽ ἑξῆς προθύμους εἶναι. Clearly, πάντας ἑξῆς in Pseudo-Xenophon is quite sound.

A more difficult text is Lucian *Verae Historiae* 1.7.75–76:

> ... ὁ ποταμός. ἦν δὲ καὶ ἰχθῦς ἐν αὐτῷ πολλοὺς ἰδεῖν, οἴνῳ μάλιστα καὶ τὴν χρόαν καὶ τὴν γεῦσιν προσεοικότας· ἡμεῖς γοῦν ἀγρεύσαντες αὐτῶν τινας καὶ ἐμφαγόντες ἐμεθύσθημεν· ἀμέλει καὶ ἀνατεμόντες αὐτοὺς εὑρίσκομεν τρυγὸς μεστούς. ὕστερον μέντοι ἐπινοήσαντες τοὺς ἄλλους ἰχθῦς τοὺς ἀπὸ τοῦ ὕδατος παραμιγνύντες ἐκεράννυμεν τὸ σφοδρὸν τῆς οἰνοφαγίας.

Among the wonders recounted by Lucian in the *Verae Historiae* is a river of wine which he tells us he found on a marvelous island in the Atlantic. In the Greek passage given above (1.7) he explains what happened when he and his men ate some fish from the river. The final sentence ὕστερον ... οἰνοφαγίας has been thought corrupt. The Teubner editor Nilén asks in his *apparatus*: "qui pisces? quae aqua?" Jaeger (*Hermes* 64 [1929] 39–40 = *Scripta Minora* 2.24–25), noting that two good manuscripts (Γ and Ω) omit τοὺς ἀπό, considered these words a "byzantinische Interpolation." He would read τοῖς ἄλλοις ἰχθύσι τοῦ ὕδατος παραμιγνύντες where the genitive τοῦ ὕδατος would be partitive = "some water." However, interpolations are usually made to clarify; to judge from the results, τοὺς ἀπὸ would be a distinctly infelicitous interpolation.

The words given in the manuscripts are sound, though perhaps obscure (the omission in a few manuscripts of τοὺς ἀπὸ is probably only a mechanical lipography: the copyist's eyes jumped from τοὺς to τοῦ). The words τοὺς ἄλλους . . . ὕδατος mean: "the other fish—in contrast to the 'wine-fish'—those, that is, which come from water." τοῦ ὕδατος with the article does not refer to some specific body of water, it means "water" as an *element*, hence the article (this seems to have misled Nilén). This same usage occurs two lines below: τὸ μὲν γὰρ ἀπὸ τῆς γῆς κτλ.

What is the sense? Jaeger rightly understood that there was a reference here to the Greek practice of tempering wine by mixing it with water. But there is a difference in this case; we are dealing with solids: an οἰνοφαγία, not an οἰνοποσία. Just as Lucian tempers liquid wine with liquid water, so here he tempers his "wine-fish" with "water-fish." (For those who demand verisimilitude of Lucian and wonder where such "water-fish" came from, he tells us in this chapter that he came upon this river when he had gone inland from the shore not much more than "three stades"; in other words, the Atlantic Ocean was less than a half mile distant.) The mixing, of course, is achieved by placing the fish on a plate side by side (παραμιγνύντες). This is a legitimate type of μῖξις, the various kinds of which were studied in great detail by the philosophers. (Compare, e.g., *SVF* 2.151 sq., Usener, *Epicurea* p. 207.12–26.) In Philo of Alexandria, for example, we read the following: ἀλλ' ἡ μὲν μῖξις ἐν ξηραῖς, ἡ δὲ κρᾶσις ἐν ὑγραῖς οὐσίαις δοκιμάζεται. μῖξις μὲν οὖν σωμάτων διαφερόντων ἐστὶν οὐκ ἐν κόσμῳ παράθεσις . . . κρᾶσις δ' οὐ παράθεσις, ἀλλὰ . . . ἀντιπαρέκτασις . . . ὡς ἐπὶ οἴνου καὶ ὕδατός φασι γίνεσθαι (*De Confus. Ling.* 184–185 = 2.264.23–25 Cohn and Wendland). This custom of serving different varieties of fish together is still practiced in Mediterranean countries; in Italian such a dish is called *fritto misto*. [This discussion of the Lucian passage was originally published in *HSCP* 67 (1963) 275–276.]

§74. Euripides *Phoenissae* 312–317

τί φῶ σε; πῶς ἅπαντα
καὶ χερσὶ καὶ λόγοισι
πολυέλικτον ἀδονὰν
[ἐκεῖσε καὶ τὸ δεῦρο]
περιχορεύουσα τέρψιν παλαιᾶν λάβω
χαρμονᾶν;

312. ἅπαντα : ἀπαντῶ Pearson : ἀπανταχοῦ Paley : ἀπαντᾷ olim Renehan   313. λόγοισι : κόμαισι Grotius, alii cum *l* (κόμῃσι, ex Hec.
v. 837) : κόραισι Musgrave   314. τ᾽ post ἀδονὰν add. Wecklein
315. ἐκεῖσε καὶ τὸ δεῦρο del. Murray

Jocasta is speaking. The chorus of Phoenician women have just in-
formed her of the arrival in Thebes, under truce, of her son Polynices
whom she has not seen for some time. She enters, sees her son, and in
agitated verses (301 sq.) asks him to embrace her. They embrace and
there follow the verses printed above, which I have given according to
Murray's text. Considering their brevity, they have their full share of
difficulties. Some notion of the various attempts to rewrite them may
be gotten from the specimen *apparatus* above. But there is considerable
truth in Murray's pronouncement: "Plus interpretationis eget...
Euripides quam emendationis." The crucial problems are four: (1) the
soundness of ἅπαντα, (2) the meaning of καὶ χερσὶ καὶ λόγοισι, (3)
ἐκεῖσε καὶ τὸ δεῦρο, which Murray deleted as having crept in from
verse 266, and (4) the construction of ἀδονὰν. I shall consider the last
question first. Scholefield construed λάβω ἀδονὰν, τέρψιν χαρμονᾶν;
most construe it with περιχορεύουσα, as does Paley, who calls it an
"irregular accusative." ἀδονὰν surely goes with περιχορεύουσα, but it
is scarcely "irregular"; it is a quite regular cognate accusative. The
only thing unusual about πολυέλικτον ἀδονὰν is that the poet has
elegantly placed the cognate notion in the adjective πολυέλικτον rather
than in the noun. Euripides couples these same two roots in *Troiades*
332–333: χόρευε, μᾶτερ, ἀναγέλασον· / ἕλισσε τᾷδ᾽ ἐκεῖσε. This

passage is also telling against Murray's deletion of ἐκεῖσε καὶ τὸ δεῦρο, for τᾷδ' ἐκεῖσε is quite parallel. There is another parallel in *Orestes* 1292: ἀλλ' αἱ μὲν ἐνθάδ', αἱ δ' ἐκεῖσ' ἑλίσσετε. Furthermore, in verse 266, the supposed source of the "interpolation," the expression is κἀκεῖσε καὶ τὸ δεῦρο, not ἐκεῖσε καὶ τὸ δεῦρο. If the words crept in from verse 266, why any change at all? Such slight variations are often significant. The change from κἀκεῖσε to ἐκεῖσε is intentional and is evidence of genuineness. Euripides had just written καὶ χερσὶ καὶ λόγοισι, in which expression καὶ ... καὶ means "both ... and" (this is certain, as will appear below). He thereupon deliberately omitted καὶ with ἐκεῖσε to avoid using καὶ ... καὶ, "both ... and," twice in such close proximity. Next let us examine καὶ χερσὶ καὶ λόγοισι ("by touching you, addressing you" Paley), which may best be considered together with ἅπαντα. What are we to make of this word? Scholefield construed περιχορεύουσα [sc. σε] ἅπαντα; what that can mean in context escapes my wit. Murray prints ἅπαντα, but in his *apparatus* writes "fortasse ἀπαντῶ." This shows that he had doubts about the word, but ἀπαντῶ is not satisfactory. Jocasta has already met Polynices at verse 304 and has been addressing him since then. The Budé editors, Grégoire and Méridier, follow Wecklein in adding ⟨τ'⟩ after ἁδονάν. They translate: "Comment, de toutes les manières, avec les mains, avec la parole, multipliant autour de toi, en tout sens, le tourbillon de ma danse ravie, retrouver le plaisir des anciennes délices?" This triad (a) χερσὶ, (b) λόγοισι, (c) πολυέλικτον ἁδονὰν ἐκεῖσε καὶ τὸ δεῦρο περιχορεύουσα is refuted by its patent imbalance. Why should the third member—the least important, be it noted—be allotted seven words instead of a simple ποσί? Professor Charles Murgia pointed out to me the correct meaning of καὶ χερσὶ καὶ λόγοισι: the words are nothing but a poetic equivalent of such common formulae as ἔργῳ καὶ λόγῳ and ἔργῳ τε καὶ ἔπει. χείρ is so used by Homer (*Iliad* 1.77), ἔπεσιν καὶ χερσίν; Sophocles *OT* 883–884 has χερσὶν ἢ λόγῳ (compare *OC* 1296–1297); see LSJ s.v. χείρ IV. (At least one scholiast understood the meaning of χείρ here: ... πῶς καὶ διὰ λόγων καὶ δι' ἔργων καὶ πανταχόσε σκιρτῶσα λάβω ἡδονὴν πολύτροπον καὶ παντοίαν, δι' ἔργου καὶ λόγου καὶ σκιρτημάτων γινομένην ... The tripartite interpretation is incorrect, though; the ἔργον / λόγος contrast in Greek is a dichotomy.)

The expression καὶ χερσὶ καὶ λόγοισι is an elegant poetic expansion which further defines the neuter plural accusative of respect ἅπαντα. This collocation of an accusative of respect and a dative of respect has been the main stumbling block to retaining the MS reading of the sentence. Wecklein compares verses 746–747 of this same play:

— θάρσει προκρίνας ἢ φρενῶν εὐβουλίᾳ;
— ἀμφότερον . . .

At verse 747 he further compares Plato *Gorgias* 477D (ἢ . . . ἀνίᾳ . . . ἢ βλάβῃ ἢ ἀμφότερα) and *Laches* 187A (ἢ δώροις ἢ χάρισιν ἢ ἀμφό-τερα). Homer has several examples of this collocation: πρεσβυτάτην . . . / ἀμφότερον, γενεῇ τε καὶ οὕνεκα σὴ παράκοιτις / κέκλημαι (*Iliad* 4.60); ἀμφότερον, φιλότητι καὶ αἰδοῖ φωτὸς ἑῆος (*Odyssey* 14.505). It may be objected that these passages are restricted to the use of ἀμφότερον (-α). The objection is invalid; they demonstrate the possibility of the crucial *construction*, the combination of the accusative and dative of respect. Nevertheless, it would be more convincing if we had a closer parallel to ἅπαντα; by chance I am able to furnish one, Ignatius of Antioch *Epistle to the Trallians* 12.1: ἀσπάζομαι ὑμᾶς ἀπὸ Σμύρνης ἅμα ταῖς συμπαρούσαις μοι ἐκκλησίαις τοῦ θεοῦ, οἳ κατὰ πάντα με ἀνέπαυσαν σαρκί τε καὶ πνεύματι. The parallel is exact: κατὰ πάντα is further explained by σαρκί τε καὶ πνεύματι, just as ἅπαντα is by καὶ χερσὶ καὶ λόγοισι. In neither author are the datives quite identical in sense with the accusatives; we are dealing with two instances of stylistic pleonasm. Ignatius uses a prepositional phrase, κατὰ πάντα, because he is writing prose; the simple accusative of respect πάντα (ἅπαντα) is mostly poetic. Some will immediately object that the usage of an apostolic father has no relevance to the usage of a fifth-century tragic poet. This is true to a degree. No one, for example, would, on the basis of Ignatius, introduce conjecturally into the text of Euripides a phrase like αἱ ἐκκλησίαι τοῦ θεοῦ. Conversely, to attempt to defend forms such as ἁδονά or χαρμονᾶν in Ignatius because of their occurrence in Euripides would be a symptom of severe derangement.

The present case is different. The question is simply whether the colloc-ation of an accusative of respect with a dative of respect is foreign to the Greek language. The evidence of any Greek author may be legiti-mately adduced; the collective testimony of Homer, Euripides, Plato, and Ignatius demonstrates adequately that the Greeks did on occasion combine the two cases. Nor is there any inherent reason why they should not have.

These verses, therefore, have, in my judgment, come down in the MSS intact; *interpretationis causa* I give here a bald version of them: "How am I in all respects, in both word and deed, to get delight from my olden joys, ⟨in expression thereof⟩ dancing hither and thither many pleasant whirls?" The Budé editors have a note on the dancing: "L'idée nous paraît étrange, venant d'une vieille femme que l'âge accable. Mais, selon la juste observation de Pearson, la danse était pour les Grecs une façon naturelle d'exprimer leurs émotions en les idéali-sant. Dans les *Troyennes*, 332 sqq., Cassandre invite sa mère, la vieille Hécube, à entrer dans la ronde et joindre sa dance à la sienne." This note oddly misses the point. (The *Troiades* passage is irrelevant; there Cassandra is chanting in an hallucinatory frenzy.) The old woman Jocasta is *not* dancing for joy. Nor can she. That, in fact, is part of her wish. She is longing for younger days when she took joy in her child-ren and could express that joy by dancing. This detail, signalized by the words πολυέλικτον ἀδονὰν ... περιχορεύουσα, is deliberately chosen by the poet to contrast with Jocasta's actual condition, as she herself depicts it, at the beginning of her address (verses 301 sq.): Φοίνισσαν βοὰν κλύουσ᾽, ὦ νεάνιδες, γηραιῷ ποδὶ τρομερὰν ἕλκω βάσιν (the order of these words is confused in the MSS, but the sense is clear). The contrast is obvious and gives the final lie to any attempts at seeing a triadic structure in this sentence. The dancing is a distinct detail to be taken by itself, not connected with καὶ χερσὶ καὶ λόγοισι. The MSS quite correctly have no copulative particle after λόγοισι.

In attempting to defend and elucidate the transmitted reading of this passage, I have deliberately refrained from adducing one more instance of the collocation of accusative and dative of respect, since the example to which I refer occurs in a passage which is itself not free from doubts.

In the optimistic belief that I have proved my case for the *Phoenissae* passage, I append here, with brief discussion, this further parallel, Pindar *Isthmian* 1.42–45:

> εἰ δ' ἀρετᾷ κατάκειται πᾶσαν ὀργάν,
> ἀμφότερον δαπάναις τε καὶ πόνοις,—
> χρή νιν εὑρόντεσσιν ἀγάνορα κόμπον
> μὴ φθονεραῖσι φέρειν
> γνώμαις.

"And if a man is expended on virtue in every impulse—in both respects, both with respect to costs and to labors—it is necessary to bring, with ungrudging thoughts, lavish praise to those who have found it [sc. ἀρετά]." The text is that of the MSS, retained by Bowra, Turyn, and Snell, among others; some have questioned the soundness of the words ἀρετᾷ κατάκειται. Hartung, for example, proposed καταθῇ τις for κατάκειται; more recently, Beattie, *CR* 67 (1963) 77–79, has proposed ἀρετὰ κατατάκει. For the general line of interpretation which I follow, see the commentaries of Fennell and Farnell. For the language, Fennell compares Xenophon *Cynegeticus* 10.8: ᾧ γὰρ ἂν προσπέσῃ [sc. ὁ ἄγριος ὗς], εἰς τοῦτον τὴν ὀργὴν κατέθετο (= "vents his anger upon"). LSJ s.v. κατάκειμαι 9, seem to me to interpret correctly: "*is expended* in every impulse *on*." As κεῖμαι is used as a passive of τίθημι in all its meanings, so too does κατάκειμαι serve as a passive of κατατίθημι. κατατίθημι very frequently means "put down as payment," "pay down" (LSJ s.v. κατατίθημι I.3.a); Pindar so uses it metaphorically, *Nemean* 7.75–76: νικῶντί γε χάριν ... οὐ τραχύς εἰμι καταθέμεν. In our passage κατάκειται= "is paid out to" (or historically more correctly, perhaps, with middle force "pays himself out to"); the image is pointed up by δαπάναις, used here in a literal sense, and possibly is continued in κόμπον ... φέρειν. See LSJ s.v. φέρω A.IV.2. The image need not be precisely as I suggest; one cannot always be exact in interpreting Pindar's poetry. What is clear is that, when one recalls that κατάκειμαι is mediopassive to κατατίθημι, there is no adequate reason to question κατάκειται here. Reservations about the soundness of this verse have been occasioned in good part by the accusative πᾶσαν ὀργάν, which, at first sight, does appear oddly coupled with κατάκειται. (See, for example, Beattie, *loc. cit.*, whose condemnation of κατάκειται πᾶσαν ὀργάν seems to me quite unjustifiable.) It is now apparent that πᾶσαν ὀργάν is the same sort of accusative as ἅπαντα in Euripides and κατὰ πάντα in Ignatius; the scholiast goes so far as to paraphrase it by πάντα τρόπον. This accusative is in turn further defined by a second accusative of respect ἀμφότερον in close combination with the datives of respect δαπάναις τε καὶ πόνοις. As in Euripides and Ignatius, so here the accusative is not exactly equated with the datives; indeed it is an unusual—but poetically elevated—turn to conceive of δαπάναι and πόνοι as ὀργαί. In sum, then, two difficult and disputed passages, Euripides *Phoenissae* 312–317 and Pindar *Isthmian* 1.42–45, their syntax once understood, are seen to be mutually supporting; the parallel constructions in each confirm the soundness of the MSS of both.

§75. Apollonius Rhodius *Argonautica* 1.976–977

Κλείτη ἐυπλόκαμος. τὴν μὲν νέον ἐξέτι πατρός
θεσπεσίοις ἕδνοισιν ἀνήγαγεν ἀντιπέρηθεν.

"ἐξέτι πατρός: 'from her father's house.' Ap. seems to use ἐξέτι here simply for ἐκ; elsewhere it always means 'even from the time of' . . ." Mooney. Schneider conjectured ἐξέτι παιδός = ἐξέτι νηπυτίης (4.791), Merkel ἐξ ἔτι πατρός, and Fränkel, while editing ἐξέτι, suggested ἕκτοθι (comparing 1.1291 σέο δ᾽ ἕκτοθι μῆτις ὄρωρεν). The soundness of ἐξέτι πατρός is confirmed by *Odyssey* 8.245: Ζεὺς ἐπὶ ἔργα τίθησι διαμπερὲς ἐξέτι πατρῶν. Apollonius is here following a practice typical of the Alexandrian poets, the use of a Homeric word or phrase with a *new* meaning. ἐξέτι πατρός is an imitation of Homer's ἐξέτι πατρῶν. So Theocritus (*Idyll* 20.19), εἴπατέ μοι τὸ κρήγυον, uses τὸ κρήγυον in the sense of τὸ ἀληθές. The adjective κρήγυος strictly means "good" or "useful"; the meaning "true" is derived from a misinterpretation of *Iliad* 1.106, μάντι κακῶν οὔ πώ ποτέ μοι τὸ κρήγυον εἶπας. For other examples of κρήγυος=ἀληθής, see LSJ s.v. 2 and Gow at Theocritus 20.19. Theocritus, Apollonius, and Lycophron use ἴσκω with the meaning "speak," "say"; its original meaning is "make like," "deem like." The confusion arose from such lines as *Odyssey* 19.203, ἴσκε ψεύδεα πολλὰ λέγων ἐτύμοισιν ὁμοῖα. LSJ s.v. νευρά state: "*string* or *cord of sinew*, in Ep. usu. *bowstring* . . . 5. wrongly taken by some,= νεῦρον, *Il.* 8.328." In Callimachus *Hymn* 6.92, ἐτάκετο μέσφ' ἐπὶ νευράς, νευράς=νεῦρα (*s.v.l.*; Pfeiffer reads μέστ' ἐπὶ νεύροις). If the passage is sound, this meaning of νευρά may well have been based on the *Iliad* passage (ῥῆξε δέ οἱ νευρήν· νάρκησε δὲ χεὶρ ἐπὶ καρπῷ, / στῆ δὲ γνὺξ ἐριπών, τόξον δέ οἱ ἔκπεσε χειρός). Some specimens of Callimachus' "interpretations" of Homeric diction are given by R. Pfeiffer, *History of Classical Scholarship* (Oxford 1968) 139–140. Nicander *Theriaca* 311 (. . . βορέαο κακὴν προφυγόντες ὁμοκλήν . . .) uses ὁμοκλή, which should mean "threat," "rebuke," in the sense of "onset," "attack." This meaning of the word may have arisen from a false interpretation of *Iliad* 16.147: πιστότατος δέ οἱ ἔσκε μάχῃ ἔνι μεῖναι ὁμοκλήν. For other examples of ὁμοκλή="attack" in postclassical epic writers, see LSJ. To judge from the statements of some scholars and lexicographers, it is apparently necessary to point out that these mis-interpretations of Homer on the part of the *learned* Alexandrian poets were for the most part quite intentional conceits, not mistakes of ignorance. For some similar Alexandrian conceits, see above, sec. 59 *ad fin*.

§76. Euripides *Heraclidae* 75–76

ἴδετε τὸν †γέροντα μᾶλλον† ἐπὶ πέδῳ
χύμενον· ὦ τάλας.

The great Dutch scholar Hemsterhuys emended γέροντα μᾶλλον to γέροντ' ἀμαλόν; he based his correction on an entry in Hesychius: ἀμαλόν· ἀπαλόν, ἀσθενῆ. Εὐριπίδης Ἡρακλείδαις δηλοῖ. The conjecture thus is confirmed by genuine ancient tradition; note that Hesychius gives the entry in the appropriate gender, case, and number. Paleographically, the change is minimal; scribes often confused λ and λλ; κρύσταλλος, for example, is very frequently written κρύσταλος in MSS (this error is one of pronunciation). As μᾶλλον is so much commoner than the poetic ἀμαλόν, false division was almost inevitable. The adjective ἀμαλός, however, occurs nowhere else in tragedy; for this reason one might rather have conjectured ἁπαλὸν here, a word which is attested several times in lyric passages of Aeschylus and Euripides, or even ἀταλὸν, which Euripides uses in a chorus of the *Electra* (verse 699, ἀταλᾶς ὑπὸ ματρός, where see Denniston). All three adjectives would give an appropriate sense here, for they are all used of young creatures and Euripides is here likening the aged feebleness of Iolaus to the helplessness of a baby. Both ἁπαλὸν and ἀταλὸν would be perfectly easy paleographical changes; the scribal neatness of ἀμαλὸν should not be permitted to outbalance weightier considerations here. For this particular confusion one may compare Aeschylus *Persae* 537, where most editors now generally print ἁπαλαῖς. Of the MSS, M and A have ἁπαλαῖς (*sic*), and F ἀταλαῖς. Paley prints ἀταλαῖς and LSJ (s.v. ἀταλός) recognize this reading as the correct one. Prienus conjectured ἀμαλαῖς, which Weil and Dindorf (see his *Lexicon Aeschyleum* s.v.) accept; ἀμαλαῖς occurred also to Hermann, but he preferred ἀταλαῖς.

In the last analysis, what makes γέροντ' ἀμαλὸν a certain conjecture is the (derivative) testimony of Hesychius. The objection that ἀμαλός is unparalleled in tragic diction is invalid: The adjective is Homeric; Euripides, as often, has gone back to Homer for his poetic vocabulary. Hemsterhuys' great merit in his treatment of this passage was not primarily mental acumen (which he possessed to a very enviable degree), but erudition. His familiarity with the Greek lexicographers— witness his edition of Pollux—was decisive here. Unusual learning has been the *sine qua non* for the healing of many an unsound passage; there follow several illustrations.

§77. Pindar *Hymn* 1, frag. 30.1-7 Snell

πρῶτον μὲν εὔβουλον Θέμιν οὐρανίαν
χρυσέαισιν ἵπποις Ὠκεανοῦ παρὰ παγᾶν

§77. *Pindar* Hymn 1

Μοῖραι ποτὶ κλίμακα σεμνὰν
  ἆγον Οὐλύμπου λιπαρὰν καθ᾽ ὁδόν
σωτῆρος ἀρχαίαν ἄλοχον Διὸς ἔμμεν·
  ἁ δὲ τὰς χρυσάμπυκας ἀγλαοκάρ-
  πους τίκτεν ἀλαθέας Ὥρας.

7. ἀλαθέας Ὥρας Boeckh : ἀγαθὰ σωτῆρας

The transmitted words ἀγαθὰ σωτῆρας in verse seven provide neither sense nor meter; Boeckh's ingenious conjecture restores both. (The meter is dactylo-epitritic; for the scheme see Snell's edition.) As Turyn suggests, the corruption may have arisen from falsely dividing the words and misinterpreting the letters σωρας as an abbreviated *nomen sacrum* = σωτῆρας. This is very possible, but not certain; the context alone was sufficient to condition a copyist to write erroneously σωτῆρας. Not only does σωτῆρος occur in the fifth verse, but Clement of Alexandria, who preserves these verses, introduces them by the following words: Πίνδαρος δὲ ἄντικρυς καὶ σωτῆρα Δία συνοικοῦντα Θέμιδι εἰσάγει, βασιλέα, σωτῆρα δίκαιον, ἑρμηνεύων ὧδέ πως. The corruption is most readily explicable if the copyist did in fact abbreviate the word σωτήρ, both scribal practice and context contributing to the corruption. Boeckh made his conjecture on the basis of a gloss in Hesychius (α 2733): ἀλαθέας ὥρας· λέγει γάρ, ὅτι κυκλισμῷ πάντα ⟨φανερὰ Bergk⟩ ποιοῦσιν. To illustrate the meaning of the phrase, Fennell compared *Olympian* 10.53–55: ὅ τ᾽ ἐξελέγχων μόνος | ἀλάθειαν ἐτήτυμον | Χρόνος; and Farnell, *Olympian* 4.1–3: Ἐλατὴρ ὑπέρτατε βροντᾶς ἀκαμαντόποδος | Ζεῦ· τεαὶ γὰρ Ὧραι | ὑπὸ ποικιλοφόρμιγγος ἀοιδᾶς ἑλισσόμεναί μ᾽ ἔπεμψαν | ὑψηλοτάτων μάρτυρ᾽ ἀέθλων. (Note especially ἑλισσόμεναι and μάρτυρ᾽.) Turyn further compares Hesychius s.v. ἀληθεῖς· οἱ μηδὲν ἐπιλανθανόμενοι, ὡς Πίνδαρος, Hesiod *Theogony* 901, δεύτερον ἠγάγετο λιπαρὴν Θέμιν, ἣ τέκεν Ὥρας, and Pindar frag. 52a.5–6 Snell, ὁ παντελὴς Ἐνιαυτός | Ὧραί τε Θεμίγονοι. There can be no reasonable doubt that Boeckh was correct in restoring Hesychius' gloss to this Pindaric fragment; the evidence is quite convincing. It is a sobering thought to reflect that it was perfectly possible, solely on the basis of the sense, Pindar's modes of thought, metrics, and paleography, to discover ἀλαθέας "Ωρας *without the aid of a Hesychian gloss.* Had any scholar done so, his would have been a brilliant emendation—but it would not have won universal acceptance.

Michigan papyrus 2754 (the so-called Alcidamas-Papyrus) reveals quite literally on what "slippery" ground the textual critic often is without realizing it:

> . . . ἀναμνησθεὶς δὲ τοῦ μαντείου ὅτι ἡ καταστροφὴ αὐτῷ τοῦ βίου ἧκεν ποιεῖ εἰς ἑαυτὸν ἐπίγραμμα τόδε· "ἐνθάδε τὴν ἱερὴν κεφαλὴν κατὰ γαῖα κάλυψε / ἀνδρῶν ἡρώων κοσμήτορα θεῖον "Ομηρον·" καὶ ἀναχωρῶν †παληου οντοσ† ὀλισθάνει καὶ πεσὼν ἐπὶ πλευρὰν οὕτως, φασίν, ἐτελεύτησεν . . .

(I have added accents, breathings, and punctuation.) We have here an account of the death of the old Homer. What is to be done with the corrupt †παληου οντοσ†? The obvious solution is to correct merely the orthography and write παλαιοῦ ὄντος: "And as he was retiring, *since he was old,* he slips . . ." Confusion of η and αι, if not the most common one, is well attested and is consonant with the level of culture of this copyist as shown by other errors (not reproduced here). Purists might prefer to make the further correction παλαιὸς ὤν, but beyond that few, I believe, would have gone, *had the papyrus text survived in isolation.* But let us suppose that someone conjectured πηλοῦ ὄντος, "because there was mud." Presented with the papyrus lection παληου and the alternatives παλαιοῦ (or: παλαιός) and πηλοῦ, which would scholars have chosen? I am speculating, of course, but it seems to me that παλαιοῦ and the *ductus litterarum* would have carried the day with the majority (and, considering the evidence, perhaps rightly!). The fact is that πηλοῦ is correct, as we know from the parallel account in the *Contest of Homer and Hesiod* (line 334 Allen; compare Tzetzes *Chil.* 13.664 Kiessling). παληου of the papyrus is in fact a misspelling for παλαιοῦ (influenced perhaps by the eta in πηλοῦ); the lection is a psychological error suggested by the context.

§78. Aeschylus *Prometheus* 829

ἐπεὶ γὰρ ἦλθες πρὸς Μολοσσὰ γάπεδα

γάπεδα Porson : δάπεδα codd. : γᾶς πέδα Weil

The meter (iambic trimeter) shows that δάπεδα of the MSS is corrupt, for that word always has a short alpha in its first syllable. Paley in his commentary observes ". . . it seems rash to deny that along with the epic δᾰπεδον, of which the etymology is uncertain, another form, δᾱπεδον, may have existed." This is unconvincing: Paley's "epic" δᾱπεδον is illusory; over and above the epic examples, Euripides has about a dozen instances of δᾰ́πεδον, and it is found also in Pindar, Aristophanes, and elsewhere. The correct etymology is given in LSJ s.v.; it is from *DM-PEDO-. The root is DEM-, DOM-, DM-,= "house"; DM- must give δᾰ- in Greek. It must be recognized, however, that, if Aeschylus believed (as Paley did) that δᾱ=γᾶ, he could have written δᾱπεδα by false etymology. The bulk of the evidence does not favor this. Weil's γᾶς πέδα (which Wecklein accepted with hesitation) seems ruled out of court by the fact that πέδον apparently was used by the poets only in the singular. Porson's γάπεδα has found almost universal acceptance. It is not at all unusual for words compounded with γη- to appear in tragedy in the so-called Doric form γᾱ-, even in nonlyric passages. Aeschylus, for example, uses γαμόρος (*Supp.* 613, *Eu.* 890), γατόμος (frag. 196.3 Nauck), γάποτος (*Ch.* 97, 164; *Pers.* 621), and Euripides uses γαπόνος (*Supp.* 420); γαπονεῖν occurs in the *Rhesus* (verse 75). For γάπεδον we have the explicit testimony of Stephanus of Byzantium s.v. Γῆ (as Porson pointed out): λέγεται καὶ γήπεδον (τὸ πρὸς τοῖς οἴκοις ἐν πόλει κηπίον), ὅπερ οἱ τραγικοὶ διὰ τοῦ ᾱ φασὶ δωρίζοντες. Stephanus' statement must be used with caution. His definition of γήπεδον as "garden" does not suit our context; this is not a refutation of Porson's conjecture, for Stephanus is merely giving a correct explanation of the one particularized meaning of γήπεδον which survived in prose (Herodotus, Plato, Aristotle). Dindorf is surely correct in assuming that γάπεδον in the tragedians was synonymous with the poetic periphrasis γῆς πέδον (see his *Lexicon Aeschyleum* s.v. γάπεδον for a lucid discussion of this passage); this would accord perfectly with the obvious etymology of the word. A passage from Lycophron's *Alexandra* (verses 615–618) provides threefold support for Porson's γάπεδα:

κολοσσοβάμων δ' ἐν πτυχαῖσιν Αὐσόνων
σταθεὶς ἐρείσει κῶλα χερμάδων ἔπι
τοῦ τειχοποιοῦ γαπέδων 'Αμοιβέως,
τὸν ἑρματίτην νηὸς ἐκβαλὼν πέτρον.

(Context: Diomedes sailed to Italy with blocks of stone from the walls of Troy in his ships as ballast; Amoebeus the wall builder is Poseidon.) The following points should be noted:

1. In cod. E (and some *deteriores*) γαπέδων has been corrupted to δαπέδων; this is a pleasant parallel for the MS corruption in Aeschylus, but this support, be it understood, was unnecessary.

2. This passage is evidence that γάπεδον was not used exclusively with the signification "garden," which it certainly does not bear here.

3. The *Alexandra* is a monologue consisting of 1474 strict *tragic* iambic verses. As regards its vocabulary, Barber (*Oxford Classical Dictionary* s.v. *Lycophron*) states "Of about 3000 words used in the *Alexandra* 518 are found nowhere else and 117 appear for the first time (Scheer). Of the rest many are 'glosses' from Epic and Tragedy, *especially Aeschylus*" (my italics).

γάπεδον occurs nowhere in the extant remains of Greek tragedy, unless Porson's restoration in the *Prometheus* is correct. (γήπεδον never occurs at all in Greek poetry.) Yet we have the express statement of Stephanus that the tragedians used the word and he was in a position to know about such matters. In view of (a) this statement and (b) the peculiar nature of the *Alexandra*, it is perfectly reasonable to conjecture that Lycophron may well have borrowed γάπεδον from the *Prometheus* (and other plays?) of Aeschylus.

The conclusion which I draw from a consideration of all the evidence is that γάπεδα should be printed in our texts of *Prometheus* 829. The conjecture ought to be regarded not as certain, but as extremely probable. We owe it to the splendid and humble learning of Richard Porson.

It has been maintained that γάπεδον should also be restored at verse 330 of Euripides' *Orestes*. Meineke in his edition of Stephanus of Byzantium s.v. *Γῆ* (p. 207.1–2 *app. crit.*) annotates, in reference to γάπεδον, "Aeschyl. Prom. 829 et Eurip. Or. 330, ubi hodie δάπεδον et δάπεδα legitur (*sic*)." This note is—I shan't say intentionally—deceptive; the normal inference to be drawn from it, in the absence of any indication to the contrary, is that Meineke himself was the first to propose γάπεδα *pro* δάπεδα in the *Prometheus* and γάπεδον *pro* δάπεδον in the *Orestes*. Meineke (1790–1870) published his *Stephanus* in 1849; Porson's edition of the *Orestes* appeared posthumously in 1811. In it at verse 324 (= verse 330 of the current editions) we read in part: "... Mox ἀνὰ τὸ δάπεδον Brunckius, addito articulo. Primam in δάπεδον producit Aeschylus Prom. 828. aut, si locus corruptus est, et hic et ibi legendum est γάπεδον. Stephanus Byz. v. *Γῆ*. λέγεται καὶ γήπεδον τὸ πρὸς τοῖς οἴκοις ἐν πόλει κηπίον, ὅπερ οἱ τραγικοὶ διὰ τοῦ α φασὶ, δωρίζοντες." It was Porson, not Meineke, who suggested γάπεδον as a possible lection for the *Orestes* passage. Here, however, the MSS all have ἀνὰ δάπεδον; ⟨τὸ⟩ was added by Brunck. Porson accepted this addition, but modern editors do not (nor, indeed, is the conjecture any longer even recorded in critical apparatuses). ⟨τὸ⟩ is superfluous and there is no reason to believe that Euripides deviated from his normal diction here. The facts are as follows: If we accept, as I think we must, that δάπεδα in the *Prometheus* is corrupt, for the simple reason that it does not scan, then neither Aeschylus nor Sophocles shows a single instance of δάπεδον in their extant remains. Euripides, on the contrary, has some dozen examples of δάπεδον. A sense of the probable can lead us in only one direction: read γάπεδα in Aeschylus and ἀνὰ δάπεδον in Euripides.

§79. Plutarch *Moralia* 364E-F (*De Iside et Osiride* 35)

ὅτι μὲν οὖν ὁ αὐτός ἐστι Διονύσῳ [sc. Ὅσιρις], τίνα μᾶλλον ἢ σὲ γιγνώσκειν, ὦ Κλέα, δὴ [?δήπου Bernardakis] προσῆκόν ἐστιν; . . . ὁμολογεῖ δὲ καὶ τὰ Τιτανικὰ καὶ †νὺξ τελεία† τοῖς λεγομένοις Ὀσίριδος διασπασμοῖς καὶ ταῖς ἀναβιώσεσι καὶ παλιγγενεσίαις.

Squire corrected the corrupt νὺξ τελεία to Νυκτέλια; the literal change is easy, but it could not have been made without some learning. Νυκτέλιος is an epithet of Dionysus; LSJ cite *AP* 9.524.14, Plut. 2.389A, Paus. 1.40.6. τὸ νυκτέλιον is a "night festival" (of Isis in *P. Oxy.* 525); the plural τὰ Νυκτέλια is used by Plutarch of the festival of Dionysus Νυκτέλιος elsewhere in the *Moralia* (291A). Wilamowitz gave a demonstration of his profound erudition in correcting a similar corruption in the *Characters* of Theophrastus (21.11):

ἀμέλει δὲ καὶ συνδιοικήσασθαι παρὰ τῶν πρυτάνεων ὅπως ἀπαγγείλῃ τῷ δήμῳ τὰ ἱερά, καὶ παρεσκευασμένος λαμπρὸν ἱμάτιον καὶ ἐστεφανωμένος παρελθὼν εἰπεῖν· "ὦ ἄνδρες Ἀθηναῖοι, ἐθύομεν οἱ πρυτάνεις [τὰ ἱερὰ] τῇ Μητρὶ τῶν θεῶν τὰ Γαλάξια, καὶ τὰ ἱερὰ καλά, καὶ ὑμεῖς δέχεσθε τὰ ἀγαθά."

τὰ ἱερὰ ante τῇ Μητρὶ del. Petersen   Γαλάξια Wilamowitz : γὰρ ἄξια V

This passage forms part of Theophrastus' account of the man who is μικροφιλότιμος, who is forever "seeking petty distinctions" (LSJ). For the technical phraseology of the proclamation, the commentators aptly compare Demosthenes (?) *Prooemia* 54:

. . . καὶ γὰρ ἐθύσαμεν τῷ Διὶ τῷ σωτῆρι καὶ τῇ Ἀθηνᾷ καὶ τῇ Νίκῃ, καὶ γέγονεν καλὰ καὶ σωτήρια ταῦθ' ὑμῖν τὰ ἱερά. ἐθύσαμεν δὲ καὶ τῇ Πειθοῖ καὶ τῇ Μητρὶ τῶν θεῶν καὶ τῷ Ἀπόλλωνι, καὶ ἐκαλλιερούμεν καὶ ταῦτα. ἦν δ' ὑμῖν καὶ τὰ τοῖς

ἄλλοις θεοῖς τυθένθ᾽ ἱέρ᾽ ἀσφαλῆ καὶ βέβαια καὶ καλὰ καὶ σωτήρια. δέχεσθ᾽ οὖν παρὰ τῶν θεῶν διδόντων τἀγαθά.

The *Galaxia* was an Athenian religious festival in honor of the
Μητὴρ θεῶν, as we learn from an entry in the Λέξεις ῾Ρητορικαί published by Bekker in his *Anecdota Graeca* (p. 229.25): Γαλαξία (*sic*):
ἑορτὴ ᾽Αθήνησι μητρὶ θεῶν ἀγομένη, ἐν ᾗ ἑψοῦσι (*leg.* ἕψουσι) τὴν
γαλαξίαν. ἔστι δὲ πόλτος κρίθινος ἐκ γάλακτος. Hesychius s.v. Γαλάξια has a similar entry. Wilamowitz' conjecture is as ingenious as it is
learned, and the explicit mention of the Μήτηρ θεῶν in Theophrastus
should have removed all doubt as to its correctness. Furthermore, only
one extant inscription makes reference to τὰ Γαλάξια (see below). This
indicates that the festival was an unimportant one; that is to say, exactly
the sort of insignificant ceremony about which a μικροφιλότιμος ἀνήρ
would trouble himself. (I owe this acute observation to Professor Ster-
ling Dow.) Most editors now print Γαλάξια, but there are still some
scholars who remain unconvinced—and they have the authority of
Jebb for their position. Lingering doubts are due, in good part, to the
disquieting presence of τὰ ἱερὰ before τῇ Μητρὶ in V (= codex Vaticanus Graecus 110), the sole MS of authority for this section of the
Characters.

The key to the explication of this passage is to be found, in my opinion,
in a careful analysis of the several meanings of θύω (LSJ are deficient in
this respect). θύω, cognate with θυμός, Latin *fumus*, etc., originally
signified to make an offering by *burning* it; it soon came to mean
"offer," "sacrifice," "slay a victim" in general. It is used both absolutely and with a direct object (namely, the offering). LSJ s.v. θύω (A)
I.4 give the further meaning "*celebrate* with offerings or sacrifices";
they cite, among others, the following examples:

βασιλέως γενέθλια πᾶσα θύει καὶ ἑορτάζει ἡ ᾽Ασία.

([Pl.] I *Alc.* 121C)

Ξενίας ὁ ᾽Αρκὰς τὰ Λύκαια ἔθυσε.

(Xen. *Anab.* 1.2.10)

τὰ ῾Ηράκλει᾽ ἐντὸς τείχους θύειν ἐψηφίζεσθε.

(Dem. 19.86)

ὁ δὲ στεφανοῦται καὶ θύει γάμους.

(Plut. *Pomp.* 55)

Other examples are:

τὰ ἐπινίκια ἔθυεν αὐτός τε καὶ οἱ χορευταί.

(Pl. *Symp.* 173A)

ἔθυε τὰ εὐαγγέλια.

(Xen. *HG* 1.6.37)

Actually, two distinct meanings of θύω can be elucidated from these examples. Neuter plural adjectives such as ἐπινίκια, εὐαγγέλια, γενέθλια, though seemingly used substantively, really agree with an understood ἱερά; the same is true of the names of the games and festivals: τὰ ᾽Ίσθμια (sc. ἱερά), τὰ Παναθήναια (sc. ἱερά), and so forth. An expression such as θύειν τὰ ἐπινίκια is literally "to offer the sacrifices in honor of a victory"; the accusative τὰ ἐπινίκια is the same accusative as in, say, θύειν πέντε βοῦς. Gradually, the connotation "celebrate," originally present only by implication, came to be the dominant one in some expressions; in the Plutarch passage cited above, θύει γάμους= "he celebrates his marriage (with appropriate sacrifices)." In the expressions θύειν βοῦς and θύειν γάμους the accusatives are not the same (or, more precisely, they are the direct objects of θύω used in two distinct senses: (1) "offer," "sacrifice," (2) "celebrate with sacrifices"). As a waggish friend of mine observed, one cannot immolate a marriage. To return now to the Theophrastus passage, the question to be asked is whether τὰ Γαλάξια had come to signify to an Athenian primarily (a) a festival or (b) offerings (ἱερά) made at a festival. The answer is clear; both the Bekker entry and Hesychius define Γαλάξια as a ἑορτή; an Attic ephebic decree of 107/106 B.C. (*IG* 2².1011.13) removes all doubt: . . . ἔθυσαν δὲ καὶ τοῖς Γαλαξίο[ι]ς τῇ Μητρὶ τῶν θεῶν . . . (= ". . . and also *at the Galaxia* they sacrificed to the Mother of the gods"). τοῖς Γαλαξίοις is a dative of time; the dative without a preposition is regularly so used with the *names of festivals* (Kühner–Gerth 1.445). The expression θύειν τὰ Γαλάξια means "to celebrate with offerings the Galaxia," not "to offer the Galaxia." Once we clarify the meaning and construction of ἐθύομεν ... τὰ Γαλάξια, it becomes immediately apparent that τὰ ἱερὰ before τῇ Μητρὶ must be regarded as an interpolation and deleted, for the very good reason that there is no verb to govern it; it is grammatically impossible here. It is easy enough to understand how τὰ ἱερὰ could have gotten into the text. In the preceding sentence the "man of petty ambition" contrives ὅπως ἀπαγγείλῃ τῷ δήμῳ τὰ ἱερά; once τὰ Γαλάξια had corrupted to τὰ γὰρ ἄξια, ἐθύομεν was left without an object (since τὰ γὰρ ἄξια appeared to be the beginning of a new sentence). Someone may have felt that ἐθύομεν needed an object and consciously added τὰ ἱερά; alternately, the words need be nothing but an accidental misplacement, possibly from the margin.

Some slight additional support for Γαλάξια may be seen in the imperfect tense ἐθύομεν. If the meaning of θύω here were primarily "sacrifice" rather than "celebrate with accompanying sacrifices," we should have expected the aorist ἐθύσαμεν, the normal tense in such formulae; compare the ephebic decree and the Demosthenic prooemium cited above. (This distinction should probably not be pressed too much.)

Finally, LSJ s.v. θύω (A) I.5 state "c. dupl. acc., εὐαγγέλια θ. ἑκατὸν βοῦς ... Ar. *Eq.* 656." This is inexact and I caution anyone against citing it as a parallel supporting ... ἐθύομεν ... τὰ ἱερὰ ... τὰ Γαλάξια construed as a "double accusative." Surely in Aristophanes εὐαγγέλια does not signify a festival; ἱερά is to be understood with it and it is *in apposition with* βοῦς: "sacrifice a hundred oxen *as* thank-offerings for the good news."

§80. Callimachus *Epigram* 44 (45)

Ἔστι τι ναὶ τὸν Πᾶνα κεκρυμμένον, ἔστι τι ταύτῃ
ναὶ μὰ Διώννσον πῦρ ὑπὸ τῇ σποδιῇ·
οὐ θαρσέω· μὴ δή με περίπλεκε. πολλάκι λήθει
τοῖχον ὑποτρώγων ἡσύχιος ποταμός·

§80. Callimachus Epigram 44 (45)

τῷ καὶ νῦν δείδοικα, Μενέξενε, μή με παρεισδύς
οὗτος †οσειγαρνης† εἰς τὸν ἔρωτα βάλῃ.

[The following discussion first appeared in *HSCP* 68 (1964) 377–378.]
For the meaningless ουτοσοσειγαρνης Bentley conjectured οὗτος ὁ
σιγέρπης from Hesychius: σιγέρπης· λαθροδάκτης. In 1870 Otto
Schneider could remark in his edition of Callimachus: "ὁσειγάρνης
Pal., quod ingeniose correxit Bentl. cum editorum omnium plausu."
More recent editors, however, tend to reject this conjecture; Wilamowitz, Cahen, and Pfeiffer all still dagger the passage. In his *Hellenistische
Dichtung* (1.173) Wilamowitz observes that "Bentleys σιγέρπης ist mit
seiner wunderbaren Gelehrsamkeit herangeholt, aber Sinn gibt es noch
nicht." Objections to σιγέρπης are apparently based on Bentley's own
interpretation of the meaning of the word: "Σιγέρπης apud Hesy-
chium λαθροδάκτης, serpens vel canis clam subrepens et morsum inferens. idem: λαιθαργοὶ κύνες, κρύφα δάκνοντες. et alibi: ληθαργὸς
κύων, ὁ προσσαίνων μέν, λάθρα δὲ δάκνων." This interpretation of
Bentley's is followed, for example, by the Loeb editor, A. W. Mair,
who accepts the conjecture and notes: "σιγέρπης Bentley from
Hesychius' σιγέρπης· λαθροδάκτης, used of a dog which fawns only to
bite." However, in lines 3 and 4 we have a comparison to a "quiet
river"; line 5 then begins τῷ καὶ νῦν—"Therefore even now . . ."—so
that it is natural to assume that the figure of a river is still being kept
up. The introduction of a "fawning dog" at this point would be inept
and inappropriate, and the rejection of σιγέρπης so understood is
correct.

I believe that Bentley's restoration is right, but that his *interpretation*
is not. Callimachus calls his ἐρώμενος a σιγέρπης, a "*silent* creeper,"
precisely because he is continuing the comparison to a "*quiet* river"
(ἡσύχιος ποταμός) creeping past. Can this interpretation of σιγέρπης
be reconciled with Hesychius' explanation λαθροδάκτης? I think not
only that it can, but that actually the explanation itself gives further
confirmation of Bentley's conjecture. λαθροδάκτης (also in the form
-δήκτης) is applied to dogs, but it need not be exclusively so used.
Antiphanes (*AP* 11.322) sarcastically refers to certain grammarians as

124

λαθροδάκναι κόριες. In Modern Greek the technical name of a certain type of spider is λαθροδήκτης. The word might be legitimately applied to any person or thing which "bites secretly." [Professor Clive Foss of Boston College kindly called my attention to the expression ... τὴν λαθρόδηκτον τοῦ Σατᾶν ξυνωρίδα, Σέργιόν φημι καὶ Στέφανον ... which occurs in the *Vita Sancti Stephani Iunioris* written in A.D.808 by a certain Stephanus, "diaconus Ecclesiae Constantinopolitanae." (See Migne, *PG* 100.1100A.) 1968.] It should be observed that under the entry σιγέρπης Hesychius makes no explicit mention of dogs; he has only one word: λαθροδάκτης. (Bentley's note, if hastily read, can be deceptive in this respect.) Elsewhere, κύων is always expressed with λαθροδάκτης. Furthermore, Phrynichus (*PS*, p. 87B) states that it is an erroneous usage to apply λαθροδήκτης to dogs: λαθαργός should be used instead. If he is correct in this, we may wonder whether a professional lexicographer (Hesychius or his source) would be likely to commit such an error. It is not at all certain, therefore, that λαθροδάκτης alone in our passage must mean *canis clam subrepens et morsum inferens*, and the fact that σιγέρπης is glossed by this word does not preclude a reference to the *river* of line 3. Still, it is obvious that λαθροδάκτης, "secret biter," and σιγέρπης, "silent creeper," are not synonyms. Why then did Hesychius—or rather his source—equate them? We possess Hesychius' work only in an abridged form preserved in a single fifteenth-century manuscript. The work ultimately derives in good part from "Spezialwörterbücher" of earlier grammarians, and consequently many entries in Hesychius' lexicon are explained on the basis of one specific passage. In its original form the work gave references to the passages in which the rare words explained occurred (compare Hesychius' prefatory letter to Eulogius), so that, had Hesychius come down to us entire, we could have seen immediately whether or not he was citing σιγέρπης specifically from this epigram of Callimachus. Nevertheless, even in its present abbreviated form the entry is sufficient to suggest that Hesychius had this very poem in view: λαθροδάκτης is an *interpretamentum* of σιγέρπης based on lines 3 and 4 (πολλάκι λήθει τοῖχον ὑποτρώγων ἡσύχιος ποταμός). The grammarian who used λαθροδάκτης here realized that Callimachus called the boy a σιγέρπης because he was comparing him to the river of lines 3–4 which "escapes notice as it eats away gradually ('eat away from below,' LSJ s.v. ὑποτρώγω) a wall." This boy, like the "quiet river," was a λαθρο-δάκτης: λαθρο- was intended to be an echo of λήθει (line 3) and -δάκτης of ὑποτρώγων (line 4). Presumably in its original full form (lost to us) this interpretation of the grammarian would have been clearer.

To conclude: not only does σιγέρπης, when properly understood, make excellent sense in this passage, but the explanation λαθροδάκτης, preserved in the grammatical tradition, seems directly inspired by lines 3 and 4 of this poem. Hesychius is of acknowledged value for recovering "glosses" corrupted or replaced in the direct manuscript tradition of Greek authors (including Callimachus), and paleographically the corruption of οσιγερπης to οσειγαρνης is readily understandable. Bentley's σιγέρπης should once more be read in our texts of Callimachus.

§81

The problem of dialect forms has received short shrift in this essay; the following illustrations from Pindar may be taken as typical:

(a) *Olympian* 9.42:

> αἰολοβρέντα Διὸς αἶσα
> αἰολοβρέντα Snell : αἰολοβρόντα

(b) *Paean* 12.9–10 (Snell):

> κελαινεφέ᾽ ἀργιβρένταν . . . Ζῆνα

(c) frag. 144 (108):

> Ἐλασίβρεντα παῖ Ῥέας
> Ἐλασίβρεντα Renehan : Ἐλασίβροντα Schneider : Ἐλασί-βροντε

(d) frag. 155 (127).1-2:

καρτερόβρεντα Κρονίδα
καρτερόβρεντα Snell : καρτερόβροντα

(e) Bacchylides 17 (16).65–66:

Κρόνιος . . . ἀναξιβρέντας.

The question is whether Pindar (and Bacchylides) employed epithets
in -βρέντης or -βρόντης or both. Aristophanes has ἐλασίβροντος
(*Equites* 626) and κεραυνοβρόντης (*Pax* 376); a Mithraic inscription
from imperial Rome (? some consider it a forgery) seems to have the
form ἀστροβρόντης (*IG* 14.998). These are all the surviving examples
of such formations known to me. (Snell suggests the tentative restoration βαρυβρέντα at Bacchylides 7.4; the papyrus has only]βαρυβρ[.)
There is no doubt that terminations in -βροντος and -βρόντης are perfectly correct Greek; what must be determined is whether or not
forms in -βρέντης were also in use. The evidence is quite adequate to
permit an affirmative answer. Papyri preserve the forms ἀργιβρένταν
and ἀναξιβρέντας (cited above); since all such compounds would
naturally have been popularly associated with βροντή, it is improbable
in the extreme that an original o was twice independently miscopied as
ε. The orthography of the papyri has the ring of authenticity. The
reality of such formations receives further confirmation from an entry
in Hesychius: βρενταί· βρονταί. (The plural indicates that Hesychius is
probably citing an actual passage; the word is not a grammarian's in-
vention.) Curiously enough, it appears that for Pindar -βρόντας, not
-βρέντας, is suspicious, despite the fact that of the four Pindaric
examples three have come down to us in -βρόντας. I myself would
print -βρέντας in all four passages, though I know full well that some
will condemn this as wild rewriting founded on a rash disregard of the
evidence. It is in fact no such thing. That Pindar and Bacchylides used
epithets in -βρέντας is as certain as such things can be. Now, the very
factor that makes a corruption of, say, ἀναξιβρόντας to ἀναξιβρέντας
utterly unlikely makes the reverse corruption extremely easy: the

mental association with βροντή (aided, of course, by the similarity of uncial ε and ο) must have been at times lethal to epithets in -βρέντας. The question really boils down to this: in Pindar's literary dialect was this highly stylized and rare type of epithet likely to have occurred in two distinct forms (-βρέντας, -βρόντας) or in one only (-βρέντας)? The latter alternative, that Pindar wrote only forms in -βρέντας, seems to me much more probable; it cannot be proved with certainty. I have proposed above that we read ἐλασίβρεντα in frag. 144 (108); in response to an inquiry of mine Bruno Snell very courteously sent me the following reply: "In Pind. fr. 144 habe ich -βροντ- stehen lassen, weil ich an die Möglichkeit dachte, dass ε zu schreiben sei, wo Ableitung von βρέμω wahrscheinlich sei, dagegen ο vielleicht belassen werden müssen, wenn βροντή zugrunde liegen konnte. Aber wahrscheinlich haben Sie recht, dass man ε überall bei Pindar u. Bakchylides drucken sollte." If ἐλασίβρεντα is correct, the credit for it should certainly go to Professor Snell, who first detected this problem of Pindaric dialect.

Another feature of Pindar's language is his use of ἐν (alongside of ἐς and εἰς) *cum casu accusativo*. LSJ, who cite only *Pythian* 2.86 for this construction in Pindar, are quite misleading in this respect. Pindar also employs ἐν with the accusative at *Pythian* 2.11, 4.258, 5.38; *Nemean* 4.68, 7.31; *Paean* 7(b).46 (Snell); frags. 75 (45).1, 108 (75).2, 119 (84).1. The reading is not certain in every one of these examples (*Nemean* 4.68, for instance, is Wilamowitz' conjecture), but the usage is undoubted and was recognized by the ancient grammarians; see Cramer, *Anecdota Oxoniensia* 1, p. 169.19: ἡ ἐν κατὰ μὲν συνήθειαν συντάσσεται δοτικῇ, κατὰ δὲ Ἀττικοὺς γενικῇ, κατὰ δὲ Βοιωτοὺς καὶ αἰτιατικῇ· οὕτως γὰρ ἔχει καὶ τὸ παρὰ Πινδάρῳ κτλ. It is obvious that there may very well be passages in Pindar where copyists have accidentally ejected ἐν and replaced it by ἐς, the regular form (even in Pindar). Consider frag. 122 (87).17–20:

ὦ Κύπρου δέσποινα, τεὸν δεῦτ' ἐς ἄλσος
φορβάδων κορᾶν ἀγέλαν ἑκατόγγυι-
ον Ξενοφῶν τελέαις
ἐπάγαγ' εὐχωλαῖς ἰανθείς.

It seems to me perfectly possible that Pindar actually wrote ἐν ἄλσος; compare frag. 75 (45).1–2:

> Δεῦτ᾽ ἐν χορόν, Ὀλύμπιοι,
> ἐπί τε κλυτὰν πέμπετε χάριν, θεοί κτλ.

and *Pythian* 5.37–39:

> Κρισαῖον λόφον
> ἄμειψεν ἐν κοιλόπεδον νάπος
> θεοῦ.

In this case the evidence does not justify the rejection of the MS lection. (We have no way of knowing, for example, how considerations of *sound* might have influenced Pindar's choice between ἐς and ἐν.) ἐς ἄλσος ought to be retained in the text, but it should be recognized that ἐν ἄλσος remains a distinct possibility which ought to be recorded in the *apparatus criticus*: "fortasse ἐν ἄλσος: cf. Py. 5.38, frag. 75 (45).1" or the like. Such uncertainties are legion in textual criticism, and we must be prepared to accept them. If they leave the intellect unsatisfied, as they will, nevertheless the recognition of genuine doubt is a closer approximation to truth than is unsuspecting credence. Nor will the serious scholar dismiss with disinterest the question whether Pindar wrote ἐν or ἐς—they are the same word etymologically—on the grounds that "it makes no difference to the sense." ἐν *c. acc.* is, in literary Greek, a very rare construction which survives only in Pindar; he employed it sparingly, and obviously with deliberation. It gives, by virtue of its infrequency of occurrence, a definite poetic coloration to a passage, a special effect which ἐς does not give and one which we are still able to appreciate. In other words, in the last analysis, the problem is not a textual one; it is rather a literary one.

§82. Euripides *Orestes* 665–667

> τοὺς φίλους
> ἐν τοῖς κακοῖς χρὴ τοῖς φίλοισιν ὠφελεῖν·
> ὅταν δ᾽ ὁ δαίμων εὖ διδῷ, τί δεῖ φίλων;

Murray's *apparatus* reads as follows: "660 (*sic*) δεῖ V et suprascr. B, item Aristot. Eth. Nic. x. 9, Mor. Magn. ii. 15, Plut. Mor. p. 68 E: cf. Σ δεῖ σε, φησίν, ἐμοῦ δυστυχοῦντος κτλ.: χρὴ rell." The variants δεῖ and χρὴ present us with a difficult choice, since both words are of very frequent occurrence in Euripides. (Some scholars—most recently Benardete in *Glotta* 43 [1965] 285–298—have drawn some very fine distinctions between the meanings of these two words. Many of these distinctions are quite valid, but I do not believe that they are of help here.) In such a case ancient citations become very valuable, but must be used with caution. Before examining them, a word about Murray's *apparatus*, which unfortunately has become a bit garbled. He has somehow combined comments which belong to two distinct verses, 660 and 667. Here are verses 660–661:

> δεῖ γὰρ σ' ἐμοῦ πράσσοντος ὡς πράσσω τὰ νῦν
> πλέον φέρεσθαι, κἀμὲ συγγνώμην ἔχειν.

The scholium cited by Murray clearly refers to these verses and cannot be adduced in support of the variant δεῖ at verse 667. There do exist several scholia to verses 665–667, but they are of no help, for they are merely prose paraphrases of the passage. When we read in one of them ... εἰδὼς ὅτι ἐν τοῖς ἀδυνάτοις δεῖ τῶν φίλων ... we cannot cite this in support of the variant τί δεῖ φίλων. It is an explanation, in normal prose, of these verses, not a citation. Another scholium states: ... δεῖ τοὺς φίλους βοηθεῖν τοῖς φίλοις ... This clearly is to be referred to verses 665–666, τοὺς φίλους ... χρὴ τοῖς φίλοισιν ὠφελεῖν, but no one would argue that this is evidence for a variant δεῖ to χρὴ in verse 666. There is one scholium, specifically to verse 667, which *seems* to be relevant: "τί χρὴ φίλων": κατὰ τί ἐστι χρεία τῶν φίλων; ἀντὶ τοῦ κατ' οὐδέν ἐστι χρεία τῶν φίλων. There can be no doubt that the man who wrote this scholium had τί χρὴ φίλων in his copy of Euripides. However, we happen to know who this man was—Manuel Moschopulus, who lived under the Byzantine Emperor Andronicus II Palaeologus (1282–1328). This scholium, therefore, is valueless for our purposes; it has not the authority of antiquity, being nothing but a Byzantine comment on a Byzantine MS. (For Moschopulus, see Dindorf's edition of the *Scholia*, vol. 1, p. xvii.) The scholia are to be disregarded; what of the *testimonia*? The reference to the *Nicomachean Ethics* (p. 1169b7–8) is from the ninth book, not the tenth (Chapouthier in his Budé edition of the *Orestes* repeats the false reference!); here is the passage:

οὕτω μὲν οὖν φίλαυτον εἶναι δεῖ, καθάπερ εἴρηται· ὡς δ' οἱ πολ-
λοί, οὐ χρή.
'Αμφισβητεῖται δὲ καὶ περὶ τὸν εὐδαίμονα, εἰ δεήσεται φίλων
ἢ μή. οὐθὲν γάρ φασι δεῖν φίλων τοῖς μακαρίοις καὶ αὐτάρκεσιν·
ὑπάρχειν γὰρ αὐτοῖς τἀγαθά· αὐτάρκεις οὖν ὄντας οὐδενὸς προσδεῖσθαι, τὸν δὲ φίλον, ἕτερον αὐτὸν ὄντα, πορίζειν ἃ δι' αὐτοῦ
ἀδυνατεῖ· ὅθεν "ὅταν ὁ δαίμων εὖ διδῷ, τί δεῖ φίλων;"

I have quoted the passage at length for several reasons. First, it begins with an instance of δεῖ and χρή used in close proximity; this is perfectly normal Greek. (For example, Pindar *Olympian* 6.27–28 χρὴ τοίνυν πύλας ὕμνων ἀναπιτνάμεν αὐταῖς· / πρὸς Πιτάναν δὲ παρ' Εὐρώτα πόρον δεῖ σάμερον ἐλθεῖν ἐν ὥρᾳ; Plato *Symp.* 173C εἰ οὖν δεῖ καὶ ὑμῖν διηγήσασθαι, ταῦτα χρὴ ποιεῖν; Plutarch *Mor.* 42B οὐ γὰρ ἐκ κουρείου μὲν ἀναστάντα δεῖ τῷ κατόπτρῳ παραστῆναι καὶ τῆς κεφαλῆς ἅψασθαι . . . ἐκ δὲ ἀκροάσεως ἀπιόντα καὶ σχολῆς οὐκ εὐθὺς ἀφορᾶν χρὴ πρὸς ἑαυτόν . . .; "Longinus" 12.5 καιρὸς δὲ τοῦ Δημοσθενικοῦ μὲν ὕψους . . . ἔνθα δεῖ τὸν ἀκροατὴν τὸ σύνολον ἐκπλῆξαι, τῆς δὲ χύσεως ὅπου χρὴ καταντλῆσαι.) Secondly, in this passage Aristotle, before quoting Euripides, has written δεῖ . . . δεήσεται . . . δεῖν . . . προσδεῖσθαι . . .; this *could* have influenced Aristotle or a copyist to have written τί δεῖ φίλων here instead of τί χρὴ φίλων. This passage tends to support the variant δεῖ in Euripides, but it cannot be regarded as decisive. The passage from the pseudo-Aristotelian *Magna Moralia* (2.15) is clearly borrowed directly from this passage of the *Ethics* and therefore cannot be used as an independent ancient witness for the variant δεῖ. The Plutarch citation (*Mor.* 68E), on the contrary, does not derive from Aristotle and is a valid witness. Thus two, not three, ancient works stand on the side of δεῖ; the verse is never quoted by an ancient author with the variant χρή. The *indirect* tradition therefore favors δεῖ.

Euripides' usage elsewhere must now be considered. As I noted above, he employs both verbs very frequently. The *Concordance* lists four other passages where δεῖ and χρή are variants (I do not vouch for the completeness of the list):

Hippolytus 41	χρὴ	LP	δεῖ	MABV
Ibid., 120	χρὴ	MABV	δεῖ	LP
Ibid., 488	χρὴ	MAV	δεῖ	LPBΣ
Rhesus 218	δεῖ	LP	χρή	V

As the *Rhesus* is of doubtful authenticity, the example from it is of little help. In the three passages from the *Hippolytus* Murray opts for χρὴ in preference to δεῖ, though the reasons for his choice are not at all clear. He is not following consistently one group of MSS, and at verse 488, where there possibly is support for δεῖ in the scholia, he rejects this variant. [Wedd at *Orestes* 667 states ". . . in later Greek χρή replaced δεῖ and so frequently gets wrongfully inserted in classical texts." This is flatly contradicted by Barrett at *Hippolytus* 41: "δεῖ ultimately ousted χρή from the spoken language (even in Menander about 17 to 1, save in the impf.), and the copyist or actor will substitute the later and more familiar word for the earlier . . ." Whether χρή or δεῖ was normally used in common parlance by later scribes, both words were so frequently encountered by them in classical texts that we can hardly regard the speech patterns of scribes as a certain criterion for determining the correct variant *in a particular passage*. A medieval copyist's habit of using δεῖ rather than χρή (or vice versa) doubtlessly tended to cause an unconscious interchange now and then. But the scribes correctly preserved the δεῖ or χρή found in their exemplar far more frequently than they accidentally ejected either. The enormous frequency of both words in classical authors precludes decisively any mechanical choice between these two variants based solely on later speech patterns.] At verse 120 Murray seems to me to have chosen very possibly the wrong variant, for in verse 117 there occurs the expression χρὴ δὲ συγγνώμην ἔχειν. If Murray has printed verses 666–667 of the *Orestes* correctly (I think he has, as will appear presently), it is reasonable to expect (but not to demand) the stylistic variation ... χρὴ ... δεῖ ... which occurs there to recur here also (χρὴ in verse 117, δεῖ in verse 120). I have already observed that this *varietas scribendi* is normal Greek. χρὴ in verse 120 would then be an unconscious replacement of its synonym δεῖ, written under the influence of χρὴ in verse 117. What conclusion is to be drawn from this examination of other passages in Euripides where δεῖ and χρή are variants? There is only one that is realistic: *non liquet*. They do not help us at all. I might underscore this by pointing out that in *Hippolytus* 117 χρὴ ... συγγνώμην ἔχειν occurs, and in *Orestes* 660–661 δεῖ ... συγγνώμην ἔχειν. In neither passage is there a variant.

One more passage in Euripides is relevant, though—*Heracles* 1338–1339:

> θεοὶ δ᾽ ὅταν τιμῶσιν, οὐδὲν δεῖ φίλων·
> ἅλις γὰρ ὁ θεὸς ὠφελῶν, ὅταν θέλῃ.

Nauck deleted these lines as an interpolation inspired by *Orestes* 667. It makes no difference whether these verses are genuine or not. Whoever wrote them, they are evidence in favor of δεῖ in *Orestes* 667.

The *vox antiquitatis*, therefore, so far as we can trace it, unanimously speaks on behalf of δεῖ. That it speaks truly can be demonstrated by a consideration which I have deliberately postponed till now: δεῖ *c. gen.* is a construction which is found *passim* in ancient Greek; χρή *c. gen.* is unexampled, except in certain MSS at this one place. (The Homeric construction of χρή *c. acc. pers. et gen. rei*—e.g. οὐδέ τί σε χρὴ ἀφροσύνης—is irrelevant; if a case is to be understood in our passage, it is the *dativus personae*, a quite regular construction with δεῖ, an unattested one with χρή. The distinction which I make here is neither accidental nor imaginary. Both verbs, in another construction, frequently take the infinitive with subject *accusative*; a *dative* sometimes occurs in place of the accusative with δεῖ, but no certain example of this case-substitution can be found with χρή. The reason for these differences in construction is probably to be seen in the fact that δεῖ is a genuine verb, while χρή, apparently, was originally a substantive.) To be sure, τί χρὴ φίλων on the analogy of τί δεῖ φίλων would not be impossible, and one could argue that χρὴ is the *lectio difficilior*. In this case the argument would serve only to add further abuse to an already overabused principle. Grammar and ancient testimony are in agreement that Euripides wrote τῖ δεῖ φίλων in *Orestes* 667. The origin of the false variant χρὴ is no further to seek than the preceding verse where Euripides had indeed written χρὴ. The scribe unconsciously repeated the synonym which he had just written, just as one of his colleagues possibly did at *Hippolytus* 120.

Cicero somewhere has written of the *scientia iuris*: *res enim sunt parvae, prope in singulis litteris atque interpunctionibus verborum occupatae*. Delete the *prope* and you have a fair description of the matter of textual criticism. Whether Euripides wrote δεῖ or χρή in a given passage is hardly of metaphysical import. But we must assume that he made a choice between them. This is sufficient justification for concerning ourselves with the problem. It made a difference to the poet; it should make a difference to us. This planet, I do not doubt, shall never want for people to despise such problems and those who try to resolve them. Such contempt is founded upon the remarkable premise that one who manifests a concern for minutiae must of necessity be both indifferent to and unequal to profound problems. The Greeks, on the contrary, in their simplicity had contrived a word to express this reverence before even the smallest truth; and that word is φιλαλήθεια. The sacred writer speaks not idly when he reminds us that ὁ ἐξουθενῶν τὰ ὀλίγα κατὰ σμικρὸν πεσεῖται.

BIBLIOGRAPHICAL NOTE

Useful lists of standard works on textual criticism and related subjects (paleography, stemmatics, etc.) may be consulted in A. Dain, *Les Manuscrits* (Paris 1964) 191–196, and in *Geschichte der Textüberlieferung der antiken und mittelalterlichen Literatur* (Zürich 1961) *Band* 1, pp. 577–580. (This latter work contains essays by H. Hunger, O. Stegmüller,

H. Erbse, M. Imhof, K. Büchner, H.-G. Beck, and H. Rüdiger.) Missing from these two lists is B. A. Van Groningen, *Traité d'histoire et de critique des textes grecs* (Amsterdam 1963); I have been unable to obtain a copy of this work. Far more important, though, than general handbooks of theory are the critical editions, articles, and books of the great textual scholars of whatever century. If I may add an autobiographical note, it seems to me that I have learned most from my practice of reading Greek (and Latin) texts with continual reference to the *apparatus criticus*. Whenever a variant or conjecture is recorded, I am in the habit of posing to myself the following queries: "Has the editor chosen the reading most likely to be correct? If so, why? If not, why not?"

INDEX LOCORUM

This index was compiled by Messrs. Stanley Ragalevsky and Philip Cleary. Passages of especial importance are marked with an asterisk.

Index Locorum

JOSEPHUS
Antiquitates Judaicae 17.63–64: p. 30

LONGINUS
frag. 7 Toup: p. 101

[LONGINUS]
De Sublimitate 4.4: pp. 24, 101
9.14: p. 101
12.5: p. 131
13.1, 14.1: p. 84
32.5: p. 65
33.5, 34.3: p. 101
39.3: p. 85
39.4: p. 84
40: p. 85

LUCIANUS
Verae Historiae 1.7.75–76*: p. 105

LYCOPHRON
Alexandra 615–618: p. 118
1365: p. 86

MARCUS AURELIUS
Meditationes 5.33.6: p. 104

MARTIALIS
Liber Spectaculorum 21.7–8*: p. 46

Martyrium Polycarpi
c. 20*: pp. 69–71
c. 22*: pp. 70–71

MAXIMUS ASTROLOGUS
415: p. 19

MELETIUS MONACHUS
De Natura Hominis, PG 64.1105B–C:
p. 27
PG 64.1291D: p. 67

MENANDER
Dyscolus 818: p. 83
frag. 59.1–5 Koerte: p. 55
59.4 Koerte: p. 54
187 Koerte: p. 54

NEMESIUS EMESENUS
De Natura Hominis, PG 40.537A–B*,
552A: p. 66

NEPOS
Miltiades 4.3: p. 69

NICANDER
Theriaca 311: p. 113

NONNUS
Dionysiaca 18.288: p. 60
28.5–6: p. 20

Novum Testamentum
Acta Apostolorum 2.11: p. 13
1 *Ep. Cor.* 14.25: p. 28
1 *Ep. Cor.* 15.33: p. 53
1 *Ep. Jo.* 5.7: p. 30
Ep. Tit. 1.12: p. 53
Ev. Matt. 6.4, 6, 18: p. 28

ORIBASIUS
3.41.15–17: p. 26

ORION
p. 107.7 Sturz: p. 88

"ORPHEUS"
Argonautica 737: p. 73

Papyri
Mich. 2754: p. 116
Oxy. 449: p. 34
525: p. 120
843: p. 7

PAUSANIAS
1.28.4: p. 68
1.40.6: p. 120
8.54–56: p. 68
9.31.4*: p. 30

PHILO ALEXANDRINUS
De Confus. Ling. 184–185: p. 106
ap. Eusebius, *PE* 8.14, p. 399: p. 62

PHILODEMUS
Volumina Rhetorica 1.286: p. 98

[PHOCYLIDES]
20, 48: p. 43

PHOTIUS
Lexicon s.v. οὐκ ἐκφρῶσιν: p. 51

Index Locorum

GENERAL INDEX